PRAISE FOR COREY GRAY

"Corey delivers a powerful message about purpose, which like a well-groomed mustache, can help shape a man's life for the better."

BRIAN MOORE, PRESIDENT, MUSTACHES FOR KIDS OMAHA

"Don't let the title fool you. Though I cannot grow a mustache and have been happily married to my high school sweetheart for over 20 years, *Grow a Mustache and Survive a Divorce* is a powerful reminder of how purpose can carry us through life's toughest moments. Whether it's for charity or personal growth, engaging in something bigger than yourself brings joy resilience, and connection."

KASEY HARWICK, CHIEF OPERATING OFFICER, DUNCAN AVIATION

"Corey takes a topic many men shy away from and breaks it down with humor, honesty, and just the right dose of masculinity. His take on finding purpose and navigating divorce makes this a must-read for both divorcees and regular dudes alike.

CHRIS MATHIASEN, HISTORIAN, FELLOW MUSTACHE GROWER

"Corey's storytelling, expertise, and experience gives an honest look at how a man must transform and expand to meet his full potential. What does it mean to be a grown ass man today? It's a topic that needs conversation and Corey gives permission to have it. This book made me stand up and say fuck yes to my masculinity. A masculinity that prioritizes love, and truth, and community."

DAN MILLER, ARMY VETERAN,
RESTAURANTEUR

GROW A MUSTACHE AND SURVIVE DIVORCE

AN ANGRY EX-HUSBAND"S ROADMAP TO RECOVERY

COREY GRAY

TACTICAL 16
PUBLISHING

CONTENTS

GROW A MUSTACHE AND SURVIVE DIVORCE

Copyright © 2025 by Corey Gray

First Edition

Published by Tactical 16 Publishing

Colorado Springs, Colorado

www.Tactical16.com

ISBN: 978-1-966413-03-5 (paperback)

ISBN: 978-1-966413-02-8 (hard cover)

INTRODUCTION

If your divorce is going great and you're getting along with your ex; if you already have a bitching mustache and all the healthy friends you could ask for; if you are excited to continue a friendship and be in your ex's life happily ever after, you can stop here. This is not your book. I'm excited for you, but these pages will not provide you with any value. You're not like us. Which is great... for you. If you're angry and none of this shit makes sense, read on. If you're pissed, broken, bogged down in shit you wished didn't matter, then this might just be the book that helps you break out of your current life and break into a better one. It's right here. It's not easy, but it is simple. Are you ready? Let's use that anger and rage for good. How? I gotchu. Let's get to work.

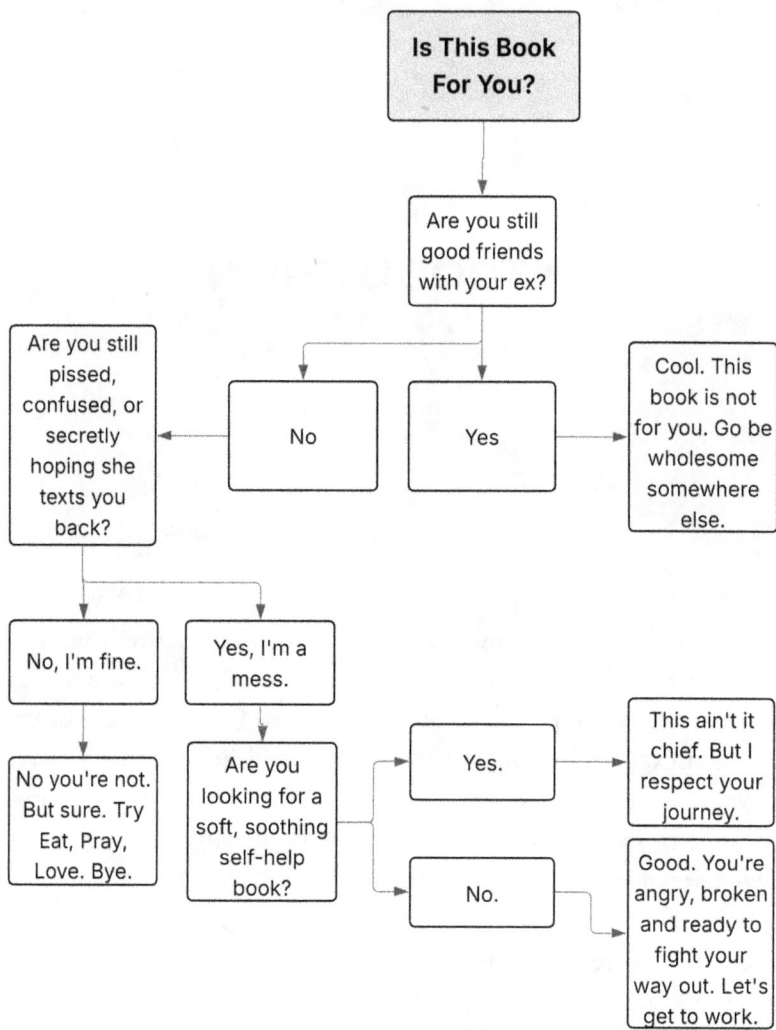

MY STORY

My family grew up poor. We struggled to stay in one house/apartment/trailer very long. We had loud, violent, angry, manipulative fights with each other. We used teasing and mean language toward one another as a way of showing affection. These relationship habits are rarely highlighted in "Successful Relationship" pamphlets. Into my 40s I've done my level best to make sense out of how my marriage ended in a nasty divorce. It took a lot to get this shit figured out. And now I'm writing this book for you.

As a 41-year-old, war veteran, former helicopter mechanic, former airplane mechanic, former college professor, current Licensed Professional Counselor who coaches high school swim & dive and runs a business; I've seen some shit. Ups. Downs. All of it. I've experienced death, injury, the loss of friends, the loss of jobs, and obviously divorce. Divorce, without a doubt, sucked the most.

I was married at 18. Went to war at 19. Had my first child at 20. I'm a first-generation bachelor's and master's degree graduate. Had my second and third kid at 23 and 26, respectively. Started my first non-profit business at 28. Got divorced at 36. Had a major career change at 38. Started a business (again) at 39. Then I turned 40... I've had the luxury of living in Europe, Asia, and all over the US. I've watched what happens in war, and I've watched people get hurt. Hell, I've hurt people. I've succeeded, and I've failed (and failed and failed). I do not think I know everything, but having a tumultuous upbringing, followed by a ragged unhealthy marriage, and continuing with a career where I sit with broken and hurt people of all genders and backgrounds to discuss why their relationships faltered; I feel like there is much I can share that you might find helpful.

If you're looking for a book with specific answers to your specific questions about your specific situation; I can't help you. If you're here because you're broken, you're hurting, and you need a place to help you organize your thoughts and emotions so you can finally piece your life back together enough to move forward; please keep going.

None of this shit is going to be easy. You're going to find that time is an asshole, people can really suck sometimes (that includes you), and anything worth doing right takes intentional and planned out hard work. I tell my kids, my swim team, and my clients the same thing I'll tell you right now, and often throughout this book. **You can do hard things**. Sometimes it is as simple as growing a mustache.

~ *Mustache Fact:*

The average mustache has about 600 hairs. That's 600 reasons to keep that upper lip majestic.

CHAPTER 1
WHERE AM I?

How the hell did you end up here? Maybe she was perfect, or she was the girl of your dreams, or they were the "person you could see yourself growing old with", and now it's all... well it's shit. She doesn't return your calls and talks shit about you to her friends, and they took your dog and put that stupid fucking sweater on it. Being alone sucks. Being alone when you thought you'd never be alone again sucks WAY more. So how did you get here?

STOP ME IF YOU'VE HEARD THIS ONE:

Your sister has a very attractive *friend* who is in the same *friend* group as you and a few buddies. You guys are always crossing paths. She makes eye contact. You make eye contact. You blush a little. She finds out you're into her; she has an epiphany that she's into you. You both have different girlfriends and boyfriends. You finally hook up and things look great. Then you have a falling out, take a "break" even though you're both not sure it was a break. You have various awkward interactions with each other, with your *friends* at the same coffee shop, with each other's new significant others. You hook up again (and again). Maybe get married in Vegas but get out of that one because alcohol is tough. Then one day she walks into your New York City apartment in the middle of your speech about not wanting her to leave only to find out you will finally be together.

Too "Ross & Rachel" for ya? Maybe *Friends* isn't your cup of tea. Maybe your relationship started more like "she likes country music" or "she likes that I wear flannel". Regardless of how it started, it doesn't fucking matter.

Relationships end. Not all of them, but most of them. Not just some, or half, MOST! 40% of first marriages end in divorce. 60% of second marriages end in divorce. Hell, all 8 of legendary radio host Larry King's marriages ended in divorce (and two of those were the same woman twice). The King of the Mustache, Tom Selleck, has even been divorced. Did you really have a chance?

THE TALE OF "EDDIE & THE CHECKLIST"

There was a guy I knew back in the Army, let's call him "Eddie". Good dude. Solid soldier. Hilarious asshole. Terrible at relationships.

See, Eddie had a *checklist* for what he wanted in a partner. He didn't write it down (or at least I don't think he did), but he had an internal checklist that governed his entire dating life. His ideal woman?

- Hot (obviously).
- Fun (but not too fun, because, you know… 'wife material').
- Loyal (because his last girlfriend cheated).
- Chill (but also deeply obsessed with him).

The problem? Eddie didn't actually *know* what a healthy relationship looked like. He had divorced parents who could barely be in the same room together (hell, they lived in different states), and most of his relationship wisdom came from movies where the guy always "wins" the girl with some grand romantic gesture like a boom box on the shoulder or by rushing in to crash the girl's wedding after recently finding out he was a prince (*spoiler: real life doesn't work that way, and your Schwartz isn't going to take you there either*).

Fast-forward: Eddie finds Ashley. Ashley is a smoke show. She's charming, funny, and checks enough boxes for Eddie to go *all in*. Within six months, they're engaged. Six. Months. He's convinced he's found *The One*.

The cracks show almost immediately because, ya see, Ashley had her own checklist, too. And Eddie? He *barely* met the minimum requirements. She wanted a man who was always emotionally available. Eddie, being a guy raised in a family where emotions were only expressed through sarcasm and hefeweizen, struggled with this.

Ashley also had a thing about social status. She loved the idea of being married to a soldier—until she realized that meant deployments, long hours, and a paycheck that wasn't funding her dream of "Instagram-worthy vacations."

Eddie, being completely blinded by the idea of love rather than the actual work of love, ignored every single red flag, and most all of the orange or yellow ones too. Two-years later Eddie is in Iraq, and Ashley is back home... with his best friend and several other dudes. Classic.

. . .

When the divorce papers came through, Eddie was *shocked*. He thought marriage was about checking all the right boxes, not about compatibility, personal growth, and actual emotional connection.

Moral of the story? Love isn't about finding someone who fits your checklist—it's about finding someone who fits your *life* and your *growth*. Also, if you have to convince yourself that someone is "The One" in the first six months, they're not. Stop it.

BLAME YOUR PARENTS!

No matter what, you were in a committed relationship with someone who was (at least for parts of it) committed to you too. You're not there anymore. You've gone through some or all the stages of relationship grief, which we will cover more later, and you're still pissed, hurt, sad, and struggling with a path through.

Here's the thing. It may not be your fault. I mean, it is (and humility is important as you read through this book), but also, let's take a minute and blame the people who raised you. Afterall, they're responsible for your disappointing Dallas Cowboy fandom and your affinity for putting Christmas lights up on October 1st (guilty...). Let's give them at least a piece of your relationship shit sandwich too.

Ideas on relationships, like learning to walk and talk and learn, are established and developed throughout your entire childhood. Sure, most relationships begin because you met through mutual friends or mutual social circles and had commonalities. Plus, you thought she was hot at some point. So you said, "fuck it" and got started. But why **those** things? Why **that** person?

. . .

Chances are it is because you saw what your parents did, or stepparents, or guardians did in their romantic relationship; sprinkled in what you saw on *Friends* and *The Bachelor* and *How I Met Your Mother* and developed a notion of connection, relationship, and attachment that slammed all those parts together. From there you likely found a person to check as many of those "awesome" boxes as possible before the red flags crept in and BAM! there you go. One big-time, fancy, overcommitted relationship. Happily ever after, right? Wrong.

What we fail to realize is that relationships have stages of development that many fail to recognize as important. We "go with the flow" and get tripped up when it doesn't look like the picture in our heads or on TV. Healthy and unhealthy, we can look at all of our romantic relationships through this lens. Mark Knapp and Anita Vangelisti developed a framework by which we can see the buildup and break down of relationships in stages. I will do my best to simplify the steps of "Coming Together" and "Coming Apart", so it is applicable to you as you read through.

Relationship Staircase:
Coming Together / Coming Apart

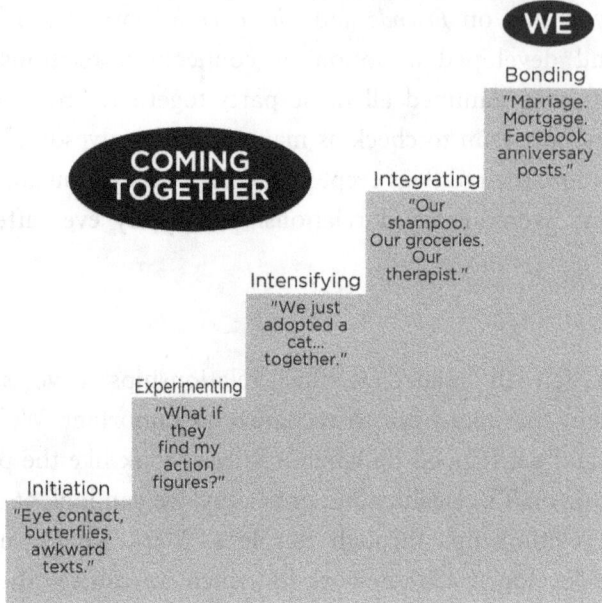

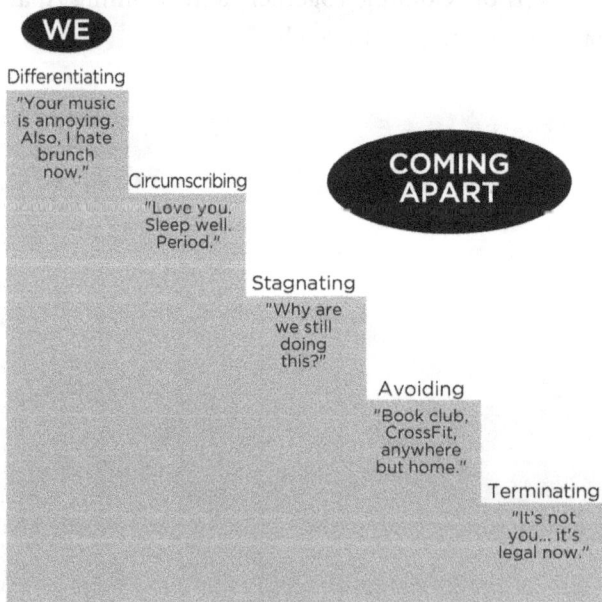

WE

COMING TOGETHER

Bonding
"Marriage. Mortgage. Facebook anniversary posts."

Integrating
"Our shampoo. Our groceries. Our therapist."

Intensifying
"We just adopted a cat... together."

Experimenting
"What if they find my action figures?"

Initiation
"Eye contact, butterflies, awkward texts."

WE

COMING APART

Differentiating
"Your music is annoying. Also, I hate brunch now."

Circumscribing
"Love you. Sleep well. Period."

Stagnating
"Why are we still doing this?"

Avoiding
"Book club, CrossFit, anywhere but home."

Terminating
"It's not you... it's legal now."

COMING TOGETHER:

- Initiation: Do we want to spend energy on seeing where this goes? Yes? Ok cool!
- Experimenting: Tell them! They're into it too, huh? How far should I go with this? What if they find my action figure collection? What if they snore (real world problems)? Eh, fuck it. Full send.
- Intensifying: When did I start to say "our" dinner instead of "my" dinner? On no. we just talked about getting a cat. This is like, REAL real.
- Integrating: "Facebook Official". We are cleaning hair out of the shower drains and popping back pimples. Maybe even peeing with the door open (you people are weird).
- Bonding: Marriage or life-partnership. Maybe children. This is that "life merge" you hear all about. Very "Mark 10:9" kind of work here, for you religious folks.

COMING APART:

- Differentiating: After years of "we" and "ours", individuals in relationships start to take back the "I" and "me" parts of their life. Finding themselves again, or for the first time.
- Circumscribing: This is the beginning of "pulling away". Fewer interactions, less texting. Maybe the previously, "I love you so much, I hope you get good sleep tonight." Becomes "Love ya, sleep well".
- Stagnating: Effortless existence. We are here, but who the hell knows where we are going.
- Avoiding: This one is easy to understand. You just avoid each other. Maybe you took on extra responsibilities at work. Or you volunteer for that community program. Maybe you take up a time-consuming hobby to get out of the house.

- <u>Terminating</u>: "It's not you, it's me". When, how, who, and various other components of ending a relationship. Rarely mutual. This is the end.

MY STORY

As mentioned, I grew up in a low socioeconomic home. My mom and dad were young, under-educated Midwestern parents. I was the oldest of three, and my mother had all of us within four years. We moved around a lot due to financial hardships or to be closer to family. I went to so many different schools before graduating from high school I can't remember them all. Things were hard for us. My mother smoked, my father struggled with his health and weight, there were periods where they struggled to hold a job for very long, and despite it all, I remember a mostly happy childhood.

My mom and dad have their own very unique way of showing love to each other. They are affectionate toward one another. They have gross nicknames and specific phrases they use on the phone before either of them hangs up ("so long" instead of "goodbye" because they believe goodbye is permanent), and both continue to talk about how much the other means to them to this day. They expressed their desire to have an intimate relationship with each other without it being "weird" or "gross". I knew they were into each other when they were getting along. My siblings and I had this version of "love" in front of us on a regular basis, and I thought it was the kind of love I wanted. At times, I really envied their relationship.

The problem with all of that is that they are also the fucking worst to each other. They would manipulate one another into getting what they wanted. They would withhold love and affection as a punishment for perceived poor behaviors. They would tease and verbally hurt the other to show "love". Gottman's Four Horsemen would have a field day with them when they engaged in marital conflict. We breakdown Gottman's Four Horsemen in much more detail in chapter nine.

My early relationships reflected many of the ups and downs I witnessed in my parent's relationship. I dated girls in high school who were affectionate and expressive with their feelings. Admittedly I dated because I wanted the status of being in a relationship and the sex that came with it. How I love others was developed by watching my parents. I developed "Words of Affirmation" and "Physical Touch" as primary Love Languages because saying "I love you" was how we knew our parents weren't mad at each other, and how we knew they weren't mad at us either. Ironically these two Love Languages are inherently the most toxic of the five. You'll find a more detailed breakdown on "Love Languages" later as well.

I did not have any other relationship role models in my childhood that I would describe as healthy. My biological grandparents were all divorced at least once. I have several aunts and uncles, almost all divorced (way to hold out Cal and Rox). However, none of their relationships would make a "healthy relationship" list. I was pretty fucked. My marriage was doomed to fail from the beginning for myriad reasons. None more important than I just didn't know any better. This could likely describe you as well. Did you know better? Like REALLY know better?

Now might be a good time to take an inventory of your own childhood and relationship role models. How did your parents or guardians love each other? How did they love you? In what ways were they excellent resources for healthy relationship traits, and in what ways did they fail you by not helping you become ready for a relationship? You're not stupid or broken because you couldn't make it work.

You're the product of your whole life and experiences. But you don't have to be anymore. After all, "Everybody is a Genius. But if you judge a fish by its ability to climb a tree, it will live its whole life believing it is stupid." Albert Einstein said that. We are not our past, but I'll be damned if our past doesn't matter.

Unless we have a good model or structure to how a healthy relationship looks and feels, we cannot expect to do it right. You can learn to be a good partner. You can learn to look for "red flags" and to implement healthy relationship boundaries. You can take classes, ask questions, read books (see? You're doing it), and you can experiment in relationships with the kind of partner you want and the kind of partner you want to be.

Chances are, if you go into your next relationship as the same person you were in your last relationship, it's going to fail again. That's not fun to hear, I'm sure. But I can assure you that the work you put into making yourself better prepared for a healthy, happy, and fulfilling relationship going forward will be SO worth it.

If it doesn't work, grow a mustache.

~Iconic Stache:
Mark Twain famously quipped, "A man without a mustache is a man without a soul."

SENSATIONALIZING AND CATASTROPHIZING

I, like many of you, can go back over the relationships that crashed and burned with a fine-tooth comb and find times where both of you were awful people. Where you moved through the "Coming Together" and "Coming Apart" stages repeatedly. Where you were in your "Trav and TayTay" Era. You might even be thinking of those things right now. You may be thinking that now is a good time to put the book down and text her? Maybe you should call her to remind her of that funny memory that will elicit a response that gives you hope again?

No. Stop. Knock it off. It's a Trap! Your brain tends to either:

- **Sensationalize** - Glorify your marriage ("It wasn't *that* bad!")
- **Catastrophize** - Demonize your marriage ("She ruined my life!")

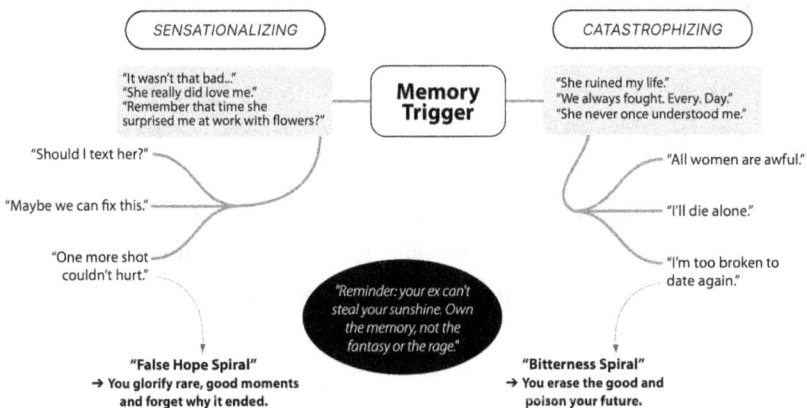

SENSATIONALIZING   CATASTROPHIZING

"It wasn't that bad..."   Memory   "She ruined my life."
"She really did love me."   Trigger   "We always fought. Every. Day."
"Remember that time she   "She never once understood me."
surprised me at work with flowers?"

"Should I text her?"   "All women are awful."

"Maybe we can fix this."   "I'll die alone."

"One more shot   "I'm too broken to
couldn't hurt."   date again."

"Reminder: your ex can't
steal your sunshine. Own
the memory, not the
fantasy or the rage."

"False Hope Spiral"   **"Bitterness Spiral"**
→ You glorify rare, good moments   → You erase the good and
and forget why it ended.   poison your future.

When relationships are coming apart, it is easy to look back on moments that bring you joy and then flip the other way to moments that bring you rage. That's just like all events in your life. It's always easy to remember the big hit in your little league game or the time you peed your pants at that frat party. In life, the highs and lows are easily recognizable. It's when we inflate them through sensationalizing and catastrophizing that we find ourselves in trouble.

· · ·

Sensationalizing happens when we take a singular positive event or memory (it might be very positive) and make that event or memory the thing that defines the entire relationship. You may find yourself saying, "Remember that time you dressed up and brought me flowers at work on my birthday? That is what our relationship was!" Or "We used to laugh together until we cried any time the dog would get lost in the blanket." These great, true, and very real memories are still great, real, and very true; but they are FAR from how the relationship looked day in and day out. These are exceptions, not norms.

Believing that an entire relationship is healthy based on infrequent positive interactions is sensationalizing within the relationship. Something that is helpful when you begin to look at these situations is to write them down. I know that journaling gets a bad rap, but here is one time where you can use it to help you through the sensationalizing of your former relationship. Write down those "epic positive moments" and then leave two blank lines under each. In those lines, write down things your partner did that hurt you. Unapologetically, truthfully, and without excuses. By seeing that there are also those negative moments, you will be able to rationalize those sensational moments and put them into a clearer context.

Notice I didn't say "forget those moments"? One common pitfall I see in clients going through sensationalizing of their relationship is that they try to turn those epic positive moments into negatives. They nitpick the event or memory, or straight up change the memory to make it seem not so great. Stop doing that. I tell clients regularly that their ex doesn't have the power to take away your sunshine.

Those memories are still awesome. Laughing at dogs is always joyful. Doing nice things for people when they least expect it is beautiful. You are incredible for those moments. Just because the person you associate with those memories hurt you, doesn't mean the memory hurt you. Stop giving them that power. They sure as shit haven't earned it.

Similar concerns can be said about catastrophizing. You've might have said, "we fight all the time" or they've said, "I never understood you". Neither of these are true. Sure, you have had times where you fought, but *all the time?* You *NEVER* understood me? Really? *EVER?* It's all bullshit. Taking the shitty things you and your partner went through in your relationship and applying it to the entirety of your relationship is simple-minded garbage. It sure as hell doesn't have a place in your recovery.

Please do not hear what I'm not saying. If you are the victim of abuse, do not look at the positives as a way to justify their behavior. I am a firm believer in the three A's of ending a relationship. Adultery, Abuse, & Addiction. Not everyone subscribes to this, which is fine, but I figured now is a good time to let you know I have been writing through that lens and will continue to do so.

WHAT NOW?

You may be sitting there saying, "at this point, it doesn't matter. It didn't work, so why are you spending so much time talking about how I see relationships when I'm not in a fucking relationship anymore!"

You're almost right. We can't fix what we've been through. We can't go back, we can't stop that fight, and we can't change how we view ourselves and our ex in that relationship. You might also be saying to yourself that relationships are off limits for the foreseeable future. These things can be true AND you can learn from them. Think of all of this like you're inventorying your toolbox and sharpening the tools you plan to use next time. No matter when, or how, or with whom next time arrives.

We can only pick up the broken pieces of ourselves and move on. I posit that moving forward is the MOST important part of all this. Sure, we should understand where things went wrong, and we will absolutely do that, but please move forward knowing that ends are not always "bad", and you will absolutely recover.

In later chapters I am going to ask you to find a way to not dwell in the past. I will never ask you to forget the past and I am a firm believer than forgiving others is not a prerequisite for recovery. I'll ask you right here and now to forgive yourself. That's the only forgiveness you are required to give.

I might also ask you to grow a mustache. Maybe. Later.

~Mustache Tip:
Beard oil isn't just for beards. Your mustache needs hydration too—show it some love.

CHAPTER 2
THIS SHIT SUCKS

BUILD A BETTER YOU

For some, you are still at the beginning of the end. Maybe you are separated and looking for a way to help you through the road ahead. For some, you've made it through everything, and it's been a while since to recognized the face in your mirror. My hope is that while you work through this chapter, you're able to come to terms with ways you can get through the end of your relationship and be a better person to yourself going forward.

As previously mentioned, time is an asshole. Some days feel like an eternity, and some days fly by. Emotions play with time like that. If you're still trying to figure out what to do now that the end here, let me help. **PUT YOURSELF (AND YOUR KIDS) FIRST**! Look, I know you are going to try and do what you think is right in the process, but I also know that when the dust settles, you're on your own. Being "nice" or "understanding" in the divorce or break up process does not serve you. She is not going to care that you were nice when she starts dating someone else (and she will). She is not going to remember how accommodating you were to her when she goes back to court for more child support because she found out you are more successful without her. You must come first. Whether you were together for a year or 20 years, you're not together anymore. While some folks are great at staying friends with their ex, it isn't near as common as many are led to believe.

Putting yourself first doesn't mean you get to be a dick. I know it is very important for me that I approach my interactions with my former partner as fair and equal as possible. It doesn't matter what benefits me or her, just what is best for the kids and what is fair. If you split time with the kids over their school holiday break, EQUAL time. If they want to go on a long vacation and you trade the time with the kids, EQUAL. You can be direct and objective and forward without being an asshole. Being an asshole feels good and is totally justifiable sometimes (don't I know it), but don't do it. There is a place for that energy, and we will cover that in the next chapter.

No matter how much sensationalizing or catastrophizing you do about your relationship, in the midst of the end you must stay objective. Stay fair and equal whenever possible.

YOUR BRAIN ON DIVORCE: THE SCIENCE OF WTF

You're not imagining it—divorce actually messes with your body chemistry. Studies show that divorce triggers the **same neural pathways as physical pain**. That means your brain literally registers heartbreak like a gunshot wound to the soul.

Your **stress hormones** are also in overdrive. Cortisol (the "stress" hormone) spikes through the roof, which is why:

- You're exhausted but can't sleep.
- Your appetite is wrecked (either stuffing your face or forgetting food exists).
- Your immune system takes a nosedive (hello, random illnesses!).
- You feel like an emotional time bomb.

And let's not even start on **dopamine and oxytocin withdrawal.** Those are the "bonding" chemicals that made your ex seem like a good idea at some point. Now that they're gone, your brain is fiending like a junkie in withdrawal.

A CHART (BECAUSE SCIENCE):

What Happens to Your Brain During Divorce?

Brain Chemical	Normal Role	Divorce Effect
Cortisol	Stress Response	Skyrockets–keeps you in "fight-or-flight mode.
Dopamine	Reward & Pleasure	Tanks–makes life feel dull and pointless.
Oxytocin	Bonding & Trust	Disappears–leaves you feeling disconnected.
Serotonin	Mood Regulation	Drops–hello, depression and mood swings!

So, when people say, "just get over it," you can confidently tell them that your new friend "science" says otherwise.

HOW I ALMOST BECAME A SWAMP MONSTER

Meet James. Let me tell you about the darkest, dumbest part of James in his "post-divorce era".

. . .

James was about two months into the process. He wasn't sleeping, he was barely eating, and James had zero motivation to do anything beyond the bare minimum to keep his job and his kids fed. His house was a disaster. Not "oh no, there are some dishes in the sink, and he needs to dust the TV stand" disaster. More like **feral raccoon den meets serial killer lair.** Laundry piles everywhere. Empty beer bottles. A fridge that contained only mustard, expired milk, bologna, and very questionable leftovers. James lived in his sweatpants. Showered MAYBE twice a week.

It wasn't that others didn't notice. His friends tried to intervene. One particularly pushy bastard (bless him) literally dragged him out of his house for a guy's night. And on the guy's night, blowing chunks into a flower planter outside of a cigar bar, James realized he was at rock bottom.

He went to a bar. A normal bar with normal, functioning adults. Meanwhile, James looked like an escaped mental patient who had forgotten how to human. His clothes barely fit because he lost 20 pounds of "divorce stress weight." His social skills were so rusty he would respond to small talk with ridiculous, overly honest statements like, "Did you know stress physically shrinks your brain?" (True, but not sexy.) To add more strife to this poor guy's night, halfway through the night, a random woman, trying to be nice, patted his arm and said, "Oh honey, are you okay?"

That was it. That was the moment James started to throw back shots, wondering if he would ever be more than someone's disgusting fucking pity project.

. . .

The next day, after recovering from the world's worst hangover, James did a thing that terrified him, much like it terrorizes a lot of adult men. He called a therapist, crying, and started getting help. It was a slow process. It started with a shower and an exorcism level cleaning of his place. But he started. James is doing much better now, but it took a lot for him to get there.

Don't be "James". Which leads me to...

~Historical Stache:
Salvador Dali styled his mustache using honey. Sticky, surreal, sensational.

HOW TO SURVIVE DIVORCE WITHOUT BECOMING A SWAMP MONSTER

You need a game plan to get through this without completely self-destructing. Lucky for you, I made a step-by-step guide. Because I care.

Step 1: Get Your Shit Together (Physically)

- **Sleep.** You can't function if you're running on fumes. If you're struggling, try melatonin, magnesium, or actually going to bed before 3 AM.
- **Eat like an adult.** Yes, divorce makes you want to survive on whiskey and Hot Pockets. Don't. Get real food. Your brain needs nutrients to rebuild.
- **Move your body.** I don't care how. Walk. Lift heavy things. Punch a heavy bag with your ex's name taped to it. Just move.

· · ·

Step 2: Build Your Crew (a full chapter coming later)

Divorce is not a solo mission. You need a crew. Not just any crew. A strategic one.

Role	Who They Are	Why You Need Them
The Therapist	A licensed professional	Because you need a neutral person who won't just tell you what you want to hear.
The "Fuck That Bitch" Friend	Your ride-or-die	This person reminds you that your ex is NOT the last woman on Earth.
The "Move On" Friend	Annoying but necessary	This one pushes you to rejoin the living world.
The Gym Buddy	The accountability partner	Someone who gets you moving when you'd rather rot in bed.

Step 3: Recognize the Grief Cycle (And Don't Get Stuck)

Yes, grief. Divorce is a loss, and you're going to go through the classic five stages of grief. The key is NOT to get stuck in any one phase.

Stage	Symptoms	Danger Zone
Denial	"We'll get back together."	Keeps you clinging to false hope.
Anger	"She ruined my life."	Fuels self-destruction (or bad emails).
Bargaining	"Maybe if I just..."	Leads to stupid decisions (do not text her).
Depression	"Nothing matters."	Isolation & self-sabotage.
Acceptance	"I'm actually okay."	Where you want to be! We'll get here.

Step 4: The Breakup Box (Why You Need One)

One of the dumbest but smartest things I did post-divorce was a breakup box.

What is this sorcery? Simple. You take everything that reminds you of your ex—photos, gifts, old love notes, her hoodie you still wear —and put it in a box. Then you:

- Burn that box (therapeutic).
- Store it in the attic or basement or the depths of hell (for future you).
- Give it to a friend to hold.

Out of sight, out of mind. It works. Sometimes not a permanent solution, but a solution none the less

MY STORY

As a 17- & 18-year-old boy, my relationship needs were typical. Since I enlisted in the Army and would be leaving the summer after I graduated high school, I wanted to have as much sex as possible before I left for basic training, and my ex-wife checked that block. She was nice, she told me I was pretty, and she did... well, the *stuff*. It wasn't a big deal, I was going to break up with her in a letter, like a coward, during the second or third week of basic training like all the recruiters told me to do... Except I didn't.

The funny thing about basic training is that it sucks so much, even mediocre attention and appreciation is HUGE. I was 18, away from home, scared, and anything that looked or sounded or felt positive was sensationalized; and red flags were easily ignored. So, when she came to my graduation for basic training at Ft. Sill, Oklahoma and told me I "should probably propose", I did just that. That's something people don't tell you about manipulation; it persists through all things. Max Weber, a founding father of Sociology, said,

"Manipulation is the dark side of charisma." For which I fell, hook, line, and marriage.

I am far from faultless in my relationship. I was married for 17 years and we both struggled regularly with mental health issues that would manifest as varying forms of poor treatment of one another. I know I wasn't an easy partner. I was angry when I came home from the war in Iraq. I was immature, selfish, and insecure. To be clear, we were terrible together. More specifically, we were terrible for each other while we were trying to grow up.

In our divorce, we are kind of the same. There were various attempts to manipulate one another into behaviors dealing with logistics and friends and family. We are both still very judgmental of the way we parent and interact with the public. We just don't like each other. Probably why we got divorced, huh?

We have spent several years raising three incredible children well above the standard for parenting while not getting along. If I am being real with you, it's been hard. That being said, I have no regrets and am unapologetic for the way I acted in the early years post-divorce. I don't forgive her for the way she treated me in our marriage and after our divorce, and I have no aspirations of forming a lasting relationship with her going forward. Even co-parenting is so difficult that we parallel parent instead (more on that later).

THE POINT

I know my story is likely different from yours, but maybe my story was the validation you needed to be able to move forward with your feelings. I know I heard repeatedly that it is important for us to find a "way to get along" and that "you have kids together, so stay nice to each other". Fuck that. I tell my clients and my kids that people have the chance to get the best out of you. You do not have to go out of your way to be a dick, but you certainly don't have to pretend the people you're forced to interact with are good people.

You want some advice to go with the "point", don't email her what you think of her. It doesn't work out and then there is a paper trail. If you're going through a divorce and the court system, be advised: the court system is far from up to date on how emotional health and intelligence works, and in most cases (probably not all) judges and attorneys will revert back to the "just get along" principle that is easy to say and horribly difficult to do. Which means when you send that "you ruined my fucking life" text, it can be used against you. Again, **STAY OBJECTIVE**. Don't editorialize, don't attack her character, and don't write things down that she can use in court or show to your children (if you have them). We will talk more about how you interact with the kids later.

GETTING TO THE END

Get a lawyer. A good lawyer.

Look, I know you're smart. I know you're capable. I know you are worried about money and your former partner is telling you how they are going to "be good" in all of this. Stop. Get a lawyer. Not just any lawyer either. Shop around. I have been through three attorneys, and I am still not sure I've found one that I feel has my best interests. Spend the money. It is worth it.

Sort out your shit.

You have likely accumulated a lot of "stuff" over the course of your relationship. It is going to be easy to say "I don't care, stuff is replace-able" until you're in a Walmart at 11pm because you don't have a fucking broom and dustpan. Your life up to this point has value. Real monetary and emotional and relational value. Make sure you split up your things with a level head and in a way that represents fairness and equal value.

Find your crew (can you tell this is important?)

We will talk at length about your support system later but spend a little time writing down who you want to keep in your life. You're about to lose friends. People are flawed and they take sides. Make your list of "must haves" and let them know. More to come on this later.

Take an inventory of yourself.

We started to do this in the last chapter and will continue to build on it going forward. If you've never made yourself a priority, now is the time. Get back into the things you love. Find new things to love. Go to the gym. Get a haircut. Get a tattoo (maybe not at first). Just get right with yourself. I'm excited to help you with this.

Find a Therapist!

Therapy is getting way more positive publicity as society understands how important it is to have good mental health, but rest assured there is still a long way to go. You're not "too broken" for therapy. Just go. Even if you have no idea how to "therapy", go anyway! I am not just pandering for love of my profession, therapists are (mostly) great at this stuff. Use www. psychologytoday.com to find a therapist in-network with your insurance that meets your needs. Oh yeah, and don't be afraid to shop around for one of these either. It's less likely you have a shitty therapist and more likely you don't fit with that provider's approach to therapy. Find your person. A good therapist in a breakup or divorce is more important than anything else on this list.

WHAT NOW?

Once you've locked these things in, it's time to live. There will be hard days (so many hard days) and there will be easy days. Ending your marriage can feel like you're dying of thirst in the desert. Emotionally, it will feel similar to the death of someone close to you. This means we grieve. Don't feel ashamed if you grieve hard either. Below is an illustration I like to use of how we use a grief model as a recovery model from divorce. Your emotions and progress through this time is going to feel a lot like a "Ball in a Box":

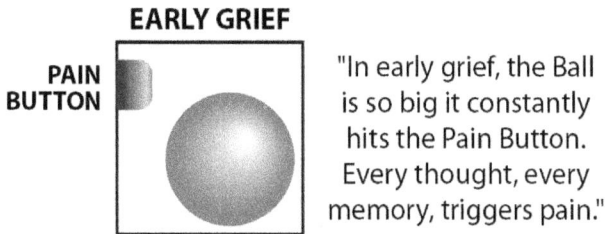

EARLY GRIEF

PAIN
BUTTON

"In early grief, the Ball is so big it constantly hits the Pain Button. Every thought, every memory, triggers pain."

In the early stages, the ball is very big. That pain you feel is massive and, at times, all you think about. It is stuck inside the "box" that is your life. You cannot move the box, meaning you cannot live without it frequently hitting the pain button. It rattles around on its own in there and hits the button over and over and over again. Sometimes it feels like nothing you do can stop that ball from smashing into the pain button and ruining your whole day.

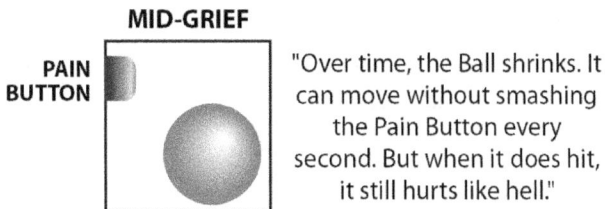

MID-GRIEF

PAIN
BUTTON

"Over time, the Ball shrinks. It can move without smashing the Pain Button every second. But when it does hit, it still hurts like hell."

But as time goes on, with a solid support system and intentional progression through the process, the ball will get smaller. It won't disappear completely, and it will still hit the pain button, just more infrequently. When it does hit the pain button again (and it will), it's just as intense. You could be having a great day. That girl from work found out you were single again and started smiling at you. You had a bomb ass chicken sandwich for lunch. Your favorite sports team is in first place in their division. Then BAM! One song that you used to associate with your ex comes on the radio and you want to literally vomit. Fuck! Why? It sucks. Smashed right into that button again.

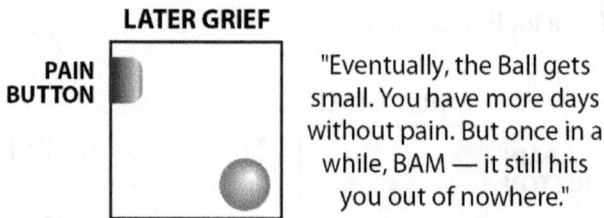

LATER GRIEF

PAIN
BUTTON

"Eventually, the Ball gets small. You have more days without pain. But once in a while, BAM — it still hits you out of nowhere."

It's not always going to be like this though. As the ball gets smaller and you fill your life with things that encourage growth and independence, that button isn't hit nearly as often. Moreover, when it does get hit, it's easier to manage because you've already survived so much. How do we get there? You're going to hate this answer, but "time" is the great victor here. You **MUST** let time go by and keep existing. That ball will shrink. It just. Takes. Time.

The analogy can help you to be able to talk about how you're feeling each day. You may say that some days the ball is a golf ball, while other days it is a fucking planet that is endlessly smashing the pain button, and you just have to wait until it gets smaller again. It is a cycle and a process.

No matter how much it hurts, or how much you want to say to your ex, or how often you feel wronged, this is not permanent. It will hurt and it will suck, and you will pray for things that will make you feel ashamed. You are not the only person in the history of the world who has felt this way. You are, however, going to come out of this as the best version of **YOU** that you've ever seen. Trust the process. We are just getting started.

~Mustache Myth:
Mustaches don't grow thicker if you shave them. Put down the razor and be patient.

CHAPTER 3
BUILD YOUR CREW

Famous Vaudeville performer turned newspaper and radio personality Walter Winchell wrote, "A real friend is one who walks in when the rest of the world walks out." In a divorce, it feels like your whole world may have just walked out, so it is time to turn your attention to those "real friends".

Last chapter I discussed the struggle of losing friends during your divorce. Data suggests you will lose 40-50% of your friends in the process. It will be easy to lose some of them, and it will be very hard to lose others. What I can promise you is that any of the friends that choose to let you go or take your ex-partners side are, for lack of a better word, assholes. This may sound like I am jaded or bitter, but I can assure you that I am not. My life, as I will share later, is better without those people in it.

Your parents told you about this exact thing since the first time you can home from school after being picked on by someone you thought was your friend. It was probably 5th or 6th grade. They sat you down, maybe told you to stop crying (not good parenting, but still likely), and said "if they don't want to be your friend, you didn't need them honey." Or some variation. Same concept applies now. You may find yourself feeling extra frustrated and angry at the friends who walk out during your divorce because it is just another relationship "lost". Like you needed to take more "L's" right now. Hang with me, and we will work through this together.

WHO STAYS AND WHO GOES?

When your marriage implodes, your social circle gets split like assets in court. Here's how to sort your friends into categories so you know who to keep close and who to let drift into the abyss.

Group 1: The "Ride or Dies"
These people are gold. They were there before, during, and after your marriage, and they will defend your honor like a medieval knight.

How to spot them:

- They don't just talk about your divorce—they talk about your life.
- They check in without being asked.
- They make you laugh, even when you feel like shit.
- They aren't interested in your ex's version of the story; they know you and they know better.

How to keep them:

- Invest in them! Friendship is a two-way street. It doesn't take much.
- Show appreciation. A simple "Hey man, I really appreciate you" goes a long way.
- Include them in your healing process. Don't just dump your trauma on them—ask about their lives too. Then don't forget to listen.

Group 2: The "Fence-Sitters"

These folks mean well, but they're afraid of picking a side. They still hang out with your ex but also check in on you occasionally. It's not that they don't care, it's that they're conflict-avoidant. Or they don't like either of you that much, you were just a good unit for them. Honestly, who knows?

How to spot them:

- They act weird around you.
- They dodge conversations about your ex.
- They make vague, half-assed statements like "I just want both of you to be happy."
- They invite you to things, but only if your ex isn't coming.

What to do with them?

- If they make an effort to support you, keep them around.
- If they're just trying to stay neutral forever, let them fade into the background.
- Don't chase them! Your time is valuable.

. . .

Group 3: The "Ex-Loyalists" (a.k.a. The Traitors)

These people jump ship the second you're single. They were either closer to your ex than you realized, or they just love drama and enjoy the spectacle of your downfall. I'd even put cowards in this category. These people super suck.

How to spot them:

- They believe every lie your ex tells.
- They suddenly stop responding to your messages.
- They say shit like, "I don't want to take sides," but they already have with their actions.
- They actively badmouth you to mutual friends or regurgitate what your ex is saying without verifying the truth.

What to do with them?

- Cut them off. Block. Delete. Erase. Bye.
- Do not engage in battles. They're not worth your energy.
- Don't let their betrayal define your self-worth. Their opinion means nothing.

Spider-Man actor Tom Holland has the perfect approach to people you should keep in your life and shared an amazing piece in an interview that I like to give to clients in session. He said, "If people have a problem with me, they can text me. If they don't have my number, they don't know me enough to have a problem with me." *Ride or Dies* will text when there is something to discuss. *Ex-loyalists* will have dinners and get togethers just to spread bullshit without ever getting your side of any story. Listen to Spider-Man.

MY STORY

After being married for 17 years at the time of my divorce, our lives were incredibly intertwined. What we owned, where we lived, our "stuff", and yes, even the people in our lives were almost all "shared" people.

Since our divorce was fast tracked and completed in four months (this is NOT normal, most divorces take a year or more. In most states it takes on average 13-18 months depending on agreeability, assets, and children) the turnover in friends worked just as fast.

I lost about six people I expected to be in my life forever. It broke me to see them enjoying their time with the person who hurt me more than any other person in the world. Watching them lean into the stories my ex shared with them about me without them reaching out to verify these stories was a kick right in the gut. These are people I trusted. And just like that, they firmly planted themselves in the "Hate Corey" tribe with my ex-wife as their Chief.

So, who stuck with me? Great question. The mutual friends who stuck with me are the best humans on the planet. The kind of people you want at your back in a foxhole when you're scared and alone and cold at war. The kind of people who watched my marriage implode under toxicity and wouldn't allow misinformation to be perpetuated without challenging it or asking me directly if the information was true.

. . .

I realize now that there are cowards and there are heroes when it comes to the equal splitting of mutual friends. Cowards are the kind of people who throw away friendships for false information, wine, and baked goods. Heroes are the kind of people who remain objective and seek the truth. Notice who your heroes are, and lock. Them. Down.

THE SCIENCE OF FRIENDSHIP DURING HARD TIMES

Humans are wired for connection. Our ancestors survived because they formed tight-knit groups. The same principle applies post-divorce. Research from the American Psychological Association (APA) shows that having a strong social support network improves resilience, lowers stress, and helps people recover from trauma faster.

Translation? Your friendships will literally keep you sane.

A study published in *Social Psychological and Personality Science* found that supportive friendships can buffer the emotional impact of breakups, making them as important as therapy (although you still need therapy, don't get cocky).

This means that who you surround yourself with isn't just a matter of "who's left" after the split. It's a critical part of rebuilding your mental health and self-worth.

Now, let's break this shit down.

~Mustache Wisdom:
"A mustache tells the world you're a man of action. Or possibly a villain. Either way, own it."

BUILDING YOUR CREW

After years of working with clients who are going through difficult divorces and learning how to survive on the back end, there is one major piece of work we do for weeks as they navigate the most painful parts of the divorce process. That is how to leverage their support system to meet their needs.

Let's face it, you're going to be A LOT during this time. Your emotions are going to be all over the place, you are going to have some wild ass ideas, and you are going to be hungry for any resemblance of positive interaction with humans. How do you get there? I would ask you to think about the people in your life that have aligned their allegiance with you, and then do the same for the things you need out of social interactions. Usually, the people you will likely need fall into the following three groups.

1. "Move On" Group
2. "You'll Both Be Better" Group
3. "Fuck That Bitch" Group

Look, not all human relationships are built from a positive place.

The "Move On" Group

This friend or group of friends has one job. Tell you regularly and often that it's "time for you to get out there" and "Don't let this hold you back", and any other made-up unhelpful thing (in the moment) they can think of because you're not as fun as you used to be. This friend, while frustrating and often wielding terrible timing, is an absolute necessity in the recovery process. It may not seem like it, but this person "want's their friend back". Fundamentally, this mean they appreciate you for the person you are, and not the relationship you were in. This is huge.

The "You'll Both Be Better" Group

This group was easily my least favorite friend in my divorce. I didn't want to hear that we were "bad for each other" (though very true), or that "it's better this way" (also true). I felt like I was "losing". This made for terrible interactions with this group. This group needs to be the group with the toughest skin, and the group that includes you in everything even though they'll tell everyone else before you get to the event to not engage with you because you're "going through it". This group is also the group you will likely lash out at most often. It sucks to hear how the person who is hurting is "good" or "better" in anyway. You will regularly and repeatedly, out loud and to yourself, say "fuck you" to this group friends. You still need them though.

The "Fuck That Bitch" Group

This, for me, was one main person, Mike, who was my go-to "FTB" guy for the duration of my divorce. I had a couple other friends in this group who were great about reminding me how awful things with my ex-wife were, but Mike was the best. These friends reminded me that there was routine manipulation and toxicity in my relationship. Only one person walked with me down my anger trail side-by-side day and night: Mike. Get yourself a Mike or two on your journey. I'm not saying this person has to actually hate your ex, they just have to let you vent and validate you the whole way. This friend doesn't ask for justification, or reasoning, or context. They rage with you and for you. You will never forget them for the role they play in this process. You might even dedicate a book to them when you make it through.

. . .

Disclaimer: Please understand that the "FTB" friend or friends are NOT to take these interactions or the information that you share outside of their interactions with you. I know several other folks who were victims of their ex's "FTB" friends. From attempting to get them fired by sending letters full of misinformation to bosses and supervisors, to having "FTB" friends anonymously spread misinformation about them on various Social Media platforms. I encourage you to find "FTB" friends who understand that hurting the other persons livelihood is a bitch move. Talking about your ex behind their back over a beer or good food, however, is a necessary piece in divorce recovery.

WHAT NOW?

Once you have these humans separated into their categories, you must let them know their role! You can't expect people to know their place in your life as you go through anything, let alone divorce. It doesn't have to be this grandiose proclamation, but rather reach out to them, sit down for coffee (good distraction tactic), and let them know you need them.

The people in your camp will not hesitate to thank you for recognizing that you are not alone, and anyone worth your friendship and time will gladly be those people for you in your life.

One more thing! You are going to be too much for some really good people if you go to the same two people over and over with the same bullshit while you are working through everything. Please spread your negativity around. Since you should have a therapist by now, they should be the person who gets the bulk of your negative self-talk and broken thoughts as you recover. Your friends are not qualified for this stuff. They are good to make sure you are eating, showering, and even good for a trash talk session, but they are not the people from which you should be taking guidance. You have a therapist for that.

Once you find your crew and let them know you need them, this whole thing gets easier. So, what's next? What else do I need to do to finally feel like I've survived this whole shit storm?

That's an easy one. Grow a Mustache and raise a million dollars!

> ~Mustache Care:
> Trim weekly, comb daily, wax proudly. A good mustache demands respect—and upkeep.

CHAPTER 4
GROW A MUSTACHE AND RAISE A MILLION DOLLARS

You have been following along and by now are wondering what the hell a Mustache has to do with surviving anything, let alone divorce. Congrats, you've made it to the Mustache chapter!

> "Efforts and courage are not enough without purpose and direction."

Senator (at the time) John F. Kennedy said this of America's current stagnation and limited capacity to "move forward" in 1960. Eventually he would be the champion for the mission to put a man on the moon. That's kind of a big deal (unless you don't think it is real, but you're dumb, so knock it off).

This process is long and grueling and mentally exhausting. You will need courage to overcome fears and you will put in a shitload of effort to move past a level of pain you've never known possible. When you run out of courage and effort, turn to purpose. We will talk about vocation and the value work will have in your recovery process in a later chapter, so this isn't about your job. It is about finding something that reminds you that there are bigger things in the world, and if you can muster up the energy and time to engage with these efforts, you'll be smacked in the face with purpose.

Finding   purpose   isn't   just   some   hokey   self-help nonsense. Psychological research backs it up: people who have a sense of purpose tend to have better mental health, higher resilience, and even live longer than those who don't. Studies show that individuals who engage in purposeful activities—even something as ridiculous as fundraising through mustache-growing—report higher levels of well-being and reduced levels of stress and depression. That's right, doing dumb shit for a good cause is scientifically proven to make you a happier human being.

But before we get too deep into the science of it all, let me tell you a story.

MY STORY

My divorce, as previously mentioned, was fast tracked. I was hood-winked and swindled every step of the way (my fault, I didn't get my own attorney until after the fact). I did have my crew and my family who were there with me the whole way. I even had my job. What I didn't have was something that gave me purpose outside of those things. Something so unrelated and new that I didn't know what I didn't know. Enter M4K...

~Mustache Fact:
In Eureka, Nevada, it's illegal for men with mustaches to kiss women. Thankfully, enforcement is lax.

MUSTACHES FOR KIDS (M4K)

Mustaches for Kids America is a nonprofit organization across the country that runs on the premise that absurdity is a prerequisite for awesomeness. M4K chapters pick one month during the year (in my location it is May) to gather weekly, grow mustaches, and raise money for children's charities in their communities.

My M4K chapter, M4K Omaha, as of writing this is the best there is. More than 250 dudes raise more than a million dollars annually for charities in the Omaha community. This group of guys are also the most supportive group of people I hang out with annually. They don't care about your political affiliation, your standing in your church, or what you do for the other 11 months a year. The only thing they care about is supporting their growers, loving their charity partners, and growing sick-ass mustaches while eating unhealthy amounts of bacon. In short, M4K was exactly what I needed.

MY STORY – CONTINUED

To really understand my story about purpose, M4K needed introduced. Sounds awesome right? It was.

My divorce went final in the month of May, and I was reeling trying to figure out what I was going to do when the final date hit. A friend of mine asked me if I had Thursdays open (which I did) and invited me to grow a mustache with him to support a non-profit organization to which he had a close connection. I was looking for anything, and the chance to get out of my small town and hang out with brand new people was perfect!

. . .

In my first year I was not a good fundraiser. My mustache was not pretty, and I was not as engaged as I would become in subsequent years, but that wasn't the purpose of M4K that first year. I got excited to go to our check-ins on Thursdays. I got excited for the presentations of the charities. To be clear, I had a new purpose. Even if it was only for a month.

We raised money that year to help children and their families to offset costs associated with cancer treatments for children. We would listen to stories about how these families were broken apart by diagnosis they did not want. Cancer sucks, and while I am not going to compare a child getting cancer to going through a divorce (not even close), I will speak to the value of contributing time and energy to something bigger than yourself while you are struggling in your own life.

I remember the exact moment when I knew I would be "ok". Each week during May, M4K has checkpoints. We get together, follow a theme or hold an event like trivia night, and hear something incredible about our charity partners. In 2019, M4K selected a non-profit organization called "Angels Among Us". Angels Among Us is a charity organization that helps offset bills for families in the community that are typically left unpaid when a child gets a serious cancer diagnosis that takes parents out of work. A damn fine organization with a brilliant group of leaders.

At one of the checkpoints, Angels Among Us allowed us to hear the story of a kid that was 9 years old. It was their third cancer diagnosis of their life, and they were there. It was WAY past the kid's bedtime, but they stood on the stage and talked about their life and what Angels Among Us had done for their family. Did I cry? Yes. Am I ashamed of crying? Fuck no. Grown men cry.

· · ·

The speech was not the "transcendent moment" though. After the speech, the group of guys I was hanging out with was at the table in the bar next to that kid's family's table. Once the kid made it back to his table, many of us were reaching out to say "hi", and to tell them how brave we thought they were. The kid, in all 9 years and 3 cancers of maturity turned to their mother and asked, "I talked to these dudes, can we go get some damn ice cream now?".

There I was. Blown away by the story and the life that kid must have lived to get through everything they have gone through. Literal years in hospitals. Pain, needles, tears, uncomfortable beds and gross hospital gowns. A revolving door of doctors and specialists, with test after test after test. Yet they stood tall, talked about their journey, thanked others for their support, and just wanted some damn ice cream. They are real life superheroes with real life problems. I was just getting divorced. I still had my job and my kids and my friends.

Because of this charity, I found a new purpose. Sure, it included hanging out with a goofy ass group of grown men who look abysmal with mustaches on their faces, but this group made me laugh on days I spent crying. They told me I was good enough on days I felt less than dirt. They told me I was welcome, and I felt like I belonged with them on days when I struggled to find my place in the world.

I didn't have cancer, and I eventually had a mustache. Talk about glass half full.

~ Stache Spotlight:
Freddie Mercury's iconic mustache defined a generation of rock —and set style standards sky-high.

WHY PURPOSE MATTERS (ESPECIALLY WHEN YOU'RE FALLING APART)

So why does all of this matter for you? Because when you're coming out of a divorce, you need a win. And that win needs to be something that isn't tied to your ex, your past, or anything else that drags you back into that pit. You need to get out of your own head and into something bigger than yourself. Research shows that people who engage in purposeful activities experience:

- Lower stress levels
- Increased resilience
- Higher life satisfaction
- Lower rates of depression
- Better cardiovascular health
- Reduced risk of cognitive decline (Yes, using your brain for something other than overanalyzing your ex's Instagram actually helps)

Below is a chart summarizing the impact of having a strong sense of purpose on various health and well-being factors:

The Benefits of Purpose in Life

Benefit	Impact
Reduced stress	Lower cortisol levels, improved emotional regulation
Increased resilience	Faster emotional recovery from setbacks
Better Physical Health	Lower risk of heart disease, improved immune function
Enhanced Mental Health	Lower depression and anxiety rates
Longer Lifespan	Increased life expectancy by 7+ years
"Turns out doing something dumb with meaning makes you happier, healthier, and harder to kill."	

WHAT NOW?

I'm not saying your thing has to be a charity organization, and I am certainly not saying that any of you will look good in a mustache. It's tricky to pull off, and the list of people who can is short (looking at you Tom Selleck). I'm merely stating that you need to find a purpose outside of your current status quo. You want to join an adult fast pitch softball league? Do it. You want to pick up a new hobby like building charcuterie boards that allows you to jump in with two feet educating yourself on wood density and its relationship to hard cheeses? Fuck yeah. Cheese it up. Just. Do. Something!

You are going to be hurting, and you are going to get sad and angry and all the other emotions that this divorce process has thrown upon you. You cannot walk around that fire, you have to walk through it. It is hot. It sucks. I can, however, tell you that detours through the fire to help others, learn a skill, or get involved with something bigger than you is a welcome pit stop along this journey.

One final pitch for M4K. There are eight chapter across the country. They all hold their mustache months at different times of the year, and they will always accept more guys. Some of them spell "Mustache" as "Moustache", which is an entirely different book on why English is a stupid language, but they are out there. If there isn't one in your area, start one! It has been six years since I started growing with these weirdos. Some of my best experiences and some of the best men and women in my life today came from finding my purpose. M4K saved me. I love you guys.

Hey man, nice mustache!

~Mustache Growth Tip:
Consistency matters. Brush regularly to encourage healthy growth and discipline unruly hairs.

CHAPTER 5
LOSING A FAMILY

In addition to losing friends, something you may not see coming is the change in family that comes along with divorce. Whether you were married for less than a year or for more than 20, your lives have overlapped so much that you may be calling her parents "mom and dad" and might have an awesome relationship with your sister-in-law or with her aunt. Whatever the situation, these extended family dynamics are changing along with everything else.

For some of the clients I work with, losing their family and the relationships that come with in-law family is very hard. It means a loss of late night bon fires or family vacations or golf buddies. I have a client who used his sister-in-law as his financial advisor before finding out his wife cheated leading to their divorce. The sister-in-law stopped talking to him and moved his money and account to someone new within her organization with a basic form email and no phone call.

.   .   .

If you have children, this becomes even more difficult. The children have relationships with these people. The kids loving spending time with their grandparents and aunts and uncles. You love this about the family. I will remind you early and often that the divorce is never a reason to punish your children. This means you must foster a working relationship with your former in-laws at times.

MY STORY

My marriage had been rocky for a while before we got divorced. That happens when you marry someone when you're still mentally a child (and I was). Both of us grew up at our own pace. I did not like the person she became. She did not like the person I became, so she called it quits. In a nutshell, that covers it. There's more to it, but that's a good basic summary.

Friends were picking sides, which sucked. I lost half of my "stuff", which is really jarring once you begin to take an inventory of what you have. I was losing a lot of the money I worked hard to earn. I felt like I was losing something almost daily for the first six months of the whole process. Like I was bleeding out with the loss of my old life.

It wasn't the friends, or the "stuff" or the time with my kids, or even the money that hurt the most. What sucked most is the members of her family I lost when they completely disconnected from me after the divorce without so much as a phone call. I understand that her family, like most, likely felt obligated, and several of them even said as much when they reached out after they heard what was going on, but I was still crushed. I have a fond memory of my father-in-law sitting me down during a fight my ex-wife and I were having at their house a couple years prior, he grabbed my hand before looking me in the eye and saying "no matter what happens, you are my family, Corey. That will never change." Then in May of 2019, the divorce was final, and he never took a call or talked to me again outside of a "hello" at my oldest daughter's high school graduation party.

He is not alone either. My former mother-in-law, who is a genuinely wonderful woman, never asked me how I felt about any of it. Before the divorce, she would spend time talking to me on the phone about her hobbies and her job, but I got nothing when it was over. We would banter about recipes, talk about our plans to travel, she would support everything I did in my career and in my pursuit of higher education. Then, all at once, I was nobody. Nothing.

My former brother-in-law and I had a wonderful friendship. We would get together and watch football on Saturday's, or go to the casino and play cards, or get together and watch our kids play together. We would support one another when my ex-wife and I were fighting (he knew what it was like to marry into the family). Again, someone I would consider a friend. Once the separation started, he went silent.

I even lost a relationship with my nephews. I held them as babies, played with them at all holidays, rooted for them in their sports and activities, and made sure they always knew I would be there for them. They were children, then all of a sudden, they were no longer "allowed" to talk to me or about me in their home. I am thankful that they still ask about me to my children, and I hope they know I will always be their biggest fan. Also, because I promised I would always be authentic while writing this book, it's really fucked up to take someone who loves and supports your children completely out of their lives. If you have been doing this because you are angry or upset, stop it. Kids need MORE people who love them. Not fewer. You're using the children to hurt people. If this sounds like you, knock it off. Be better.

Look, I know people do things they feel are in their best interests and they do things to avoid conflict or hard feelings. It is developmentally and evolutionarily part of all of us. What I didn't understand is how I could be "part of the family" for 17 plus years and then be dismissed without a phone call. I try to apply perspective to everything still today. Would I even reach out to the former partner of my child if they were in my life for 17 years? Would I challenge my own son or daughter in those moments or blindly follow whatever they told me just to make them happy? Maybe I would cut their ex off too, I don't know. I understand that it is certainly an option they had. It just sucked.

I have been able to keep a couple relationships within her family. They are very clear that I am not to tell her we still talk, and they are great about reminding me how much better things have gotten for me since ending the marriage. I am also very accommodating when it comes to their time with my kids on my parenting time (or at least I try to be). I lost a family, and that was very hard. I am also very grateful for these people for many reasons they've accumulated throughout my life.

~Historical Stache:
President William Howard Taft had the last presidential mustache. Politics hasn't recovered since.

THE SCIENCE OF FAMILY ESTRANGEMENT

Family estrangement after divorce is common, but understanding the psychology behind it might help you navigate it. Research suggests that in-law relationships are often "contingent ties." That means they exist because of the primary relationship (your marriage). When the marriage dissolves, these ties break because they were never as strong as they seemed.

According to a 2022 study published in the *Journal of Divorce & Remarriage*, around 70% of divorced individuals experience some level of estrangement from their former in-laws. Of those, 40% reported that the loss of those relationships was harder than losing friends. Why? Because, in some cases, the former in-laws were more supportive than their own families.

PERCENTAGE OF ESTRANGED IN-LAW RELATIONSHIPS POST-DIVORCE

Relationship Type	% of Estranged Relationships Post-Divorce
Father-in-law	65%
Mother-in-law	72%
Siblings-in-law	68%
Extended Family (Aunts, Uncles, Cousins)	50%
"Turns out 'you're like a son to me' expires once the paperwork hits."	

NOW WHAT?

Remember how I told you to make a list of friends and put them into categories? Do this with in-laws too. Here is the easy breakdown:

1. **The Cut-and-Run Crew:** These are the ones who drop you like a bad habit. Don't waste energy on them.

2. **The Kids' Connection Crew:** These are the ones you maintain a civil relationship with for the sake of the kids.
3. **The Ride-or-Dies:** These are the rare ones who stay in your life, even if only in secret. Fight for them, but don't expect miracles.

Some of them you will be fine to lose. Maybe they didn't hold very much value to you during your relationship, or maybe they are toxic (I have a few of those). Take that list of people, smile, and write them off like bad debt. There will come a moment when you must realize that you are the villain in their story, and you have to embrace that. Villains are sexy.

Next, look at the people you need to keep around out of necessity or for the kids (if you have kids). These are people who have done a decent job of holding the line of neutrality during the divorce or separation. Maybe you want them to be able to come to big events for the kids on your time, or you want them to ask you if they can pick up the kids for a bit to take them shopping and the only times that work are on your parenting time. These are good things! The people on this list are not there to be your friends. They exist because they are a neutral party who add value to other aspects of your life. Do NOT "throw out the baby with the bath water", even if the bath water (your ex) has to go!

Finally, pick out the people you want to fight for. These are the people you are not willing to part ways with just because your marriage didn't work. If they are folks you would consider a friend regardless of relationship, fight for them. Let them know what they mean to you and be there. It will be awkward for everyone; divorce is like that. It will not, however, be awkward forever. If these people are important to you, and you see that they are good for your life post-divorce, fight for them.

You will need to plan for difficult conversations with and about all of these people. Maybe your divorce is like mine and the adults on her side will do whatever she tells them to do out of fear that she will retaliate, and you will not have much of a choice. Maybe you will find that your in-laws have integrity and are willing to look at the situation outside of your ex's influence. Regardless, do not set expectations and then not discuss them with all parties involved. Resentment is born of unmet expectations; but that's on you if you choose to not clearly state your expectations. I am hopeful you have these conversations. They're worth it.

Boundaries will be paramount during the divorce or separation process. You need them clarified and implemented. Especially early on, you may not want people in your circles talking about your ex or talking to your ex about you. Make your wishes clear. Have ways to get out of conversations if discussions are looking like they are heading in the direction where you talk about one of those off-limits topics. It may feel unorthodox to establish communication ground rules for people with which you've had long-standing relationships but do it. Avoid the fall out later by doing the hard work up front. You can do hard things.

~Mustache Insight:
Your mustache reflects your personality. Bold. Classy. Slightly inappropriate.

CHAPTER 6
SHOW UP AND DO YOUR JOB

For some or many of you, this entire process feels like your world is imploding. You cannot gather your ducks into the same room, let alone get them in a row. Mornings come too fast thanks to nightmares or shitty dreams. Nights sneak up on you. Your days can feel incredibly short, and your place in the world is something you might be regularly questioning. I've said it before, but here goes again: divorce sucks! Where can you find joy? Purpose? Anything that doesn't fucking hurt? Maybe do your job.

In addition to leaning into your friends, your family, and finding a purpose outside of your former groups; your actual job can be an asset throughout this experience. For many folks going through divorce, their job is the only thing that didn't change. In your world, everything looks new and different. While the new and different will eventually settle out to be incredibly positive, right now you might need something that isn't so damn different. Look no further than your job! You have coworkers that rely on you for things that have no connection to your marriage. Finally! Getting to enjoy any aspect of your life without the immediate ramifications of the divorce will feel great. Go to work. Work your ass off. Be valuable. Make money. Money buys happiness (I will argue with you about this).

Research on employment and mental health is definitive! It's equally (though quite differently) valuable in this recovery process as therapy and boundaries. Please go to therapy, but it's good to know that valuable employment engenders self-reliance and leads to other real-world outcomes, including self-confidence, the respect of others, personal income, and your ability to feel a part of a community.

THE SCIENCE BEHIND WORK AND MENTAL HEALTH

Research backs this up. A 2019 study published in the *Journal of Occupational Health Psychology* found that maintaining steady employment during a major life transition significantly reduces stress, depression, and anxiety. Why? Structure, purpose, and financial stability—three things you desperately need right now.

Take a look at this chart from a study on post-divorce mental health:

Impact of Employment on Divorce Recovery

Depression & Anxiety Scores Post-Divorce
(Employed vs. Unemployed)

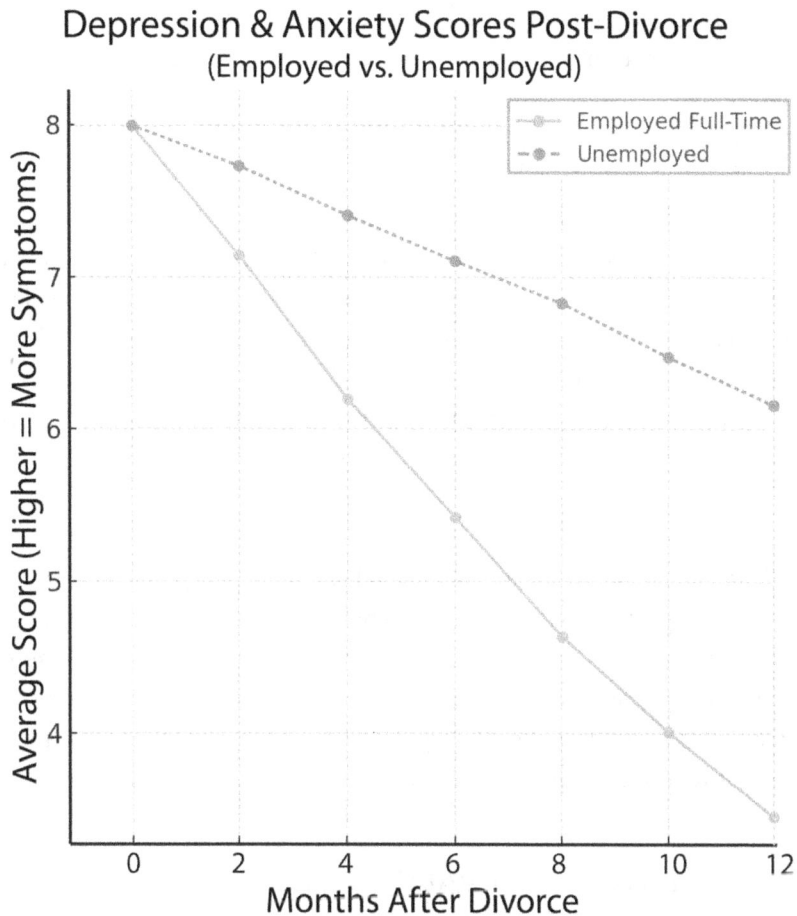

You see that? Having a job isn't just about paying bills, it's about keeping your mind from spiraling into the abyss. It doesn't work 100% of the time, and there might be days when you need to take a mental health day but trust the process.

WHY WORK MATTERS MORE THAN EVER

1. Structure and Routine Save You from Yourself
Without structure, your post-divorce life could devolve into

sleeping until noon, wearing the same sweatpants for five days, and binge-watching *Yellowstone* until your couch has a permanent indentation shaped like your ass. Work forces you to get up, shower (hopefully), and interact with humans who aren't your divorce lawyer or your therapist.

2. Financial Independence = Personal Freedom

Nothing fuels resentment like financial dependence. If your ex was the breadwinner, now is your chance to reclaim your autonomy. The more control you have over your finances, the less power they have over you. And if you were the breadwinner? You're already getting gouged for alimony and child support—so yeah, keep that paycheck rolling in.

3. Work Can Be a Distraction (In a Good Way)

You're emotionally cooked, and your brain is constantly rehashing your past mistakes at full volume. Work gives you something else to focus on. It's one of the few places where your personal drama doesn't have to take center stage. Hell, you might even have a team in place that helps you through it. I know I'm still thankful for mine.

THE TIME WORK LITERALLY SAVED MY LIFE

My divorce had just been finalized. I was still processing the fact that I was no longer legally bound to the woman who had once covered my eyes while I was driving while she was in a drunken fit of rage. Super fun times.

Anyway, the divorce happened, and I was working as a college career director at the time. The job wasn't glamorous, but it was stable and had some pretty fun times. It gave me a paycheck, gave my kids health insurance, and more importantly, gave me a reason to get out of bed.

. . .

One day, a student walked into my office for career advice (as they tend to do). He was a veteran like me, struggling to reintegrate into civilian life. He sat down, looked at me, and said, "I feel like I've lost everything."

I nodded, scoffed, and replied, "Yeah, man. Same. I get it."

For the next hour, I helped him map out a plan to get back on his feet. At the end of the conversation, he stood up, shook my hand, and said, "Thanks. I actually feel like I can do this." Super soft and feely stuff. I loved it.

That moment hit me like a truck. Here I was, barely keeping my shit together, and yet I had just helped someone else feel like they could rebuild their life. Work didn't just distract me from my own problems, it reminded me that I still had value. That I could still help people. That I wasn't just a divorce statistic. And that realization? That shit was powerful.

~Mustache Etiquette:
Soup, coffee, beer foam—check your stache before leaving the table. Nobody wants leftovers.

MY STORY

To say I have had an eclectic professional journey would be a VAST understatement. At 17-years-old I enlisted in the US Army. At 18-years and 20 days old, I left for basic combat training at Ft. Sill, Oklahoma. 27 days after that? September 11th, 2001. Talk about a crazy first two months of adulthood huh? Where was I going? War? That wasn't my plan. I was just there for the college money. What the hell?

I spent just short of six years on active duty in the US Army and had a variety of jobs. I had an occupational specialty of UH-60 Blackhawk Helicopter Repairer. I enjoyed being a mechanic and a crew chief. I flew thousands of flight hours, many in a combat zone and under night vision goggles. I served in this capacity throughout a 15-plus month deployment to Baghdad, Iraq. I thought I had an incredibly badass job.

Once I was promoted to a non-commissioned officer (E-5), I was put in charge of my Aviation Life Support Equipment (ALSE) shop in Savannah, Georgia where I supervised a mix of soldiers and civilians. As a leader, I had a lot to learn. I was a 21-year-old kid with a rank earned in the desert. I wouldn't be a good leader until much later in my professional life.

In 2006, I separated from the US Army (Honorably) and took a job as an airplane mechanic while I worked through my undergraduate college coursework. After four years working on corporate airplanes, I moved into a human services role helping unemployed veterans find work as a member of the Nebraska Department of Labor. While there, my neighbor and I started a non-profit organization called Support, Educate, & Reintegrate Veterans Everywhere (SERVE). We would hold major hiring events in the state of Nebraska to help unemployed veterans make networking connections with hiring managers in various vocational fields that would hopefully lead to their hiring. The goal being to help my brothers and sisters find their place in the working world.

.   .   .

From here, I finished my master's degree, our non-profit was dissolved due to a reduction in need in our community, and I went looking for my next "adventure". I took a job as a Career Counselor at a small parochial liberal arts college in a small Nebraska town where I would stay for the next decade. This is where my divorce would happen. I am incredibly grateful for my staff and colleagues for how they would accommodate my harder days, while also holding me accountable to my performance. Having a job while I went through my divorce gave me a reason to get up, shower, and be present with the students and my team on a daily basis. I had deadlines to meet, reports to write, and students to help. While it would've been easy for me to fold and let these things crumble alongside my marriage, the people around me at work helped me see the world as much bigger than my life at home.

Since my divorce, I have found a new calling in life. I, like many of you, have come to realize that various parts of my marriage were holding me back professionally. One of my favorite parts of being divorced is realizing how successful I could be if I followed my dreams and aspirations. I have started my own business where I employ an incredible team of professionals who share my passion for helping my community. I have watched my earnings increase to the point where I can employ my children, I can expand my services to more communities, and I can travel to show my kids the world!

I'm successful in spite of my setbacks. I know you can be too.

GRANDPA CHET

My Grandfather, Chester Weiland (Grandpa Chet), was a man I looked up to throughout my formative teenage years. He had brilliant advice, and if you could look through the subtle racism, was the kind of man who knew his place in the world of work and embraced it. He said two things I have carried with me that I would love to share with you.

First, he would say "Corey, if you show up and do what you're told, people will pay you in money." I know, No Shit, right? But at the very core of this statement is the simplicity in all of this. It really is just showing up and doing your damn job. I am aware that there is work-place politics, and a fair percentage of folks do not enjoy their job, but that doesn't mean the statement of showing up and doing your job still doesn't have application in the divorce recovery process. You are already going to be reestablishing the matrix system by which you measure your value during this process, and there is no better place to start than "Can I go to work and do what I am told?" When you answer "yes", you will be adding value to your own self-worth on a daily basis. Notice I didn't say "go above and beyond" or "build a new gadget/fidget and revolutionize your business". Just go to work. Simply do your job. Please do not hear what I am not saying, it might be hard. Simple and easy are not the same.

Second, Grandpa Chet would tell me, "Corey, you can teach a Monkey to do anything, you just have to like the Monkey." How fucking brilliant and simple is that? Grandpa was a lineman for the electric company for his entire post-military career. He climbed polls in all seasons of Iowa weather well into his 60s and he loved his job. People around loved working with him. He was likable. Our conversations about my work life always had an undertone that prodded and poked at me putting aside my Ego (I have one, you have one, we all do) and being likable enough to make people want to take chances on me.

He and I would work for hours in his woodshop where he would teach me how to build drawers using dovetail joints. He would use colorful language when I would fuck up a nice piece of oak, and I would watch him gather himself to reteach me. I guess he thought I was likable. I miss him.

Grandpa Chet's Rules for Work (and Divorce Recovery)
Because Sometimes All You Need Is a Wrench and a Good Attitude

RULE #1:
Show up and do what you're told.

"You want to feel valuable? Start by being reliable."

"Nobody cares what you're going through if you don't clock in."

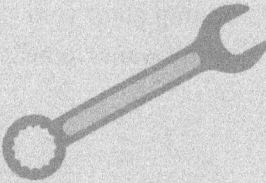

RULE #2:
You can teach a monkey to do anything...

"...but you gotta like the monkey."

"Don't be a dick. Be likable enough to get hired and rehired."

"Simple ain't easy. But it still works."
– Grandpa Chet

NOW WHAT?

1. Show Up and Do the Damn Work

This isn't the time to half-ass it. Your boss doesn't care (even though they should) that you just lost 50% of your assets and a lifetime of emotional investment. Your job is to show up, be competent, and prove to yourself that you can still function like a grown up.

. . .

Bonus: excelling at work right now gives you a sense of control when everything else feels like utter chaos.

2. Set Career Goals (Even Small Ones)

Now might not be the time for a major career shift (unless you absolutely hate your job, in which case, why not?). But setting short-term goals can keep you focused. Maybe it's earning a promotion, learning a new skill, sitting through a webinar for advancement, or just making it through the week without fantasizing about throwing a stapler at your dipshit coworker who won't stop talking about her perfect marriage.

3. Use Work as a Social Outlet (Within Reason)

Office friendships can be a lifeline. Having a work buddy to grab lunch with or to commiserate about that stupid new policy can make your days more bearable. Just don't trauma-dump all of your divorce details on your unsuspecting coworkers. Nobody wants to hear about your custody battle during a corporate retreat.

4. If You Hate Your Job, Consider a Career Change

If your job is making your post-divorce life even worse, maybe it's time to reassess. You're already rebuilding your life—why not your career?

Industries Hiring Post-Divorce:

- **Tech:** High-paying and remote options. You might need some training here.
- **Trades:** Electricians and plumbers make bank with zero to minimal office drama.

- **Healthcare:** Demand is always high, and job security is rock solid.
- **Entrepreneurship:** If you've got a passion, now's the time to build something for yourself.

WHAT ABOUT SIDE HUSTLES?

If you're looking to fill time, build confidence, or make some extra cash, a side hustle isn't the worst idea. Just don't let it turn into a full-on crisis where you think you have to pour your life into it. Maybe avoid microbreweries or forging swords until you and your therapist sign off.

Great Side Hustles Post-Divorce:

- Freelancing (writing, graphic design, consulting—whatever you're good at)
- Selling stuff online (declutter your life AND make money)
- Fitness training (since you're probably hitting the gym and getting jacked anyway)

Keep it simple. If it adds more stress than it relieves, it's not worth it. Back away slowly.

Fundamentally, your job is a place where you can escape most of the divorce bullshit. Hell, the divorce is a great opportunity for you to bury yourself in work to gain back the self-worth you've been missing in your marriage. No one said you have to like your job to be good at it. In fact, liking your job is not a requirement for showing up, doing your job, getting paid, or being likable. Wake up, shower, put on your work attire, and take your ass to work. If your divorce is gross and ugly, and let's face it, you're reading this book because it is, work might be the only place where you feel valued for a while. There and at therapy. Have I said "go to therapy" enough yet?

Besides, that new mustache will lead to so many promotions and a copious amount of workplace envy amongst your coworkers.

~*Mustache Health:*
Mustaches filter pollen and allergens. Your face is basically growing a health supplement.

CHAPTER 7
THE MINDFUCK OF DATING AFTER DIVORCE

So, you've crawled out of the wreckage of your divorce. You're bruised, battle-worn, and probably questioning everything. Asking yourself if dating is even worth it! Maybe you're bitter, maybe you're lonely, or maybe you're just fucking horny. Either way, the thought of putting yourself back out there is terrifying. Maybe your libido woke up one day and was like, "Hey, dipshit, we need to fix this dry spell." But guess what? You're not dead yet. And if you're here, that means some part of you is at least curious about what comes next. Your brain, your ego, and your baggage are all coming along for the ride, whether you like it or not. Let's break it down.

DIVORCE SCRAMBLES YOUR BRAIN—HERE'S WHY THAT MATTERS

Look, divorce isn't just a breakup—it's a goddamn identity crisis. Research says it's one of the most stressful life events you can go through, ranking just below the death of a spouse. That's right, your nervous system registers divorce like a fucking funeral, except the corpse is your former happily-ever-after, and it still occasionally texts you about the kids.

. . .

Dr. Bruce Fisher, in *Rebuilding: When Your Relationship Ends*, laid out the emotional stages people go through post-divorce: denial, anger, bargaining, depression, and finally, acceptance. These should sound familiar because we discussed the grief cycle earlier. That roller-coaster doesn't exactly make you a prime candidate for a healthy, thriving relationship. If you're still stuck in the "I hope my ex chokes on a piece of bread" phase, you're not ready to date. If you think getting laid will magically erase your pain, it will; briefly. And it will be fun; hopefully. But you're still not ready. Take a breath. Handle your shit first.

YOUR ATTACHMENT STYLE IS SCREWING WITH YOU

Ever wonder why you or some of your friends keep dating the same brand of emotionally unavailable train wreck? It's probably your attachment style, which was basically programmed into you by your parents and every shitty relationship you've ever had. See? We can keep blaming your parents a little while longer.

Here's the quick and dirty breakdown of attachment:

- **Secure Attachment**: You're chill. You communicate well. You're not scared of intimacy. You'll be fine, mostly. Probably not where you're at right now.
- **Anxious Attachment**: You fall fast, ignore red flags, turn red flags into orange ones to avoid conflict, and overanalyze text messages like a conspiracy theorist. Slow the fuck down.
- **Avoidant Attachment**: You get freaked out when people get too close and suddenly "need space." You might be better off just getting a dog first.

. . .

Figuring out your attachment style before dating again can save you from repeating past mistakes. If your ex was a walking red flag and you still find yourself attracted to their doppelgängers, that's not fate, that's bad programming. Fix it.

THE REBOUND, IS IT A BAD IDEA?

Depends. If you're using someone just to fill the void your ex left behind, yeah, that's fucked up. But if you're clear-headed and just looking for a fun, no-pressure fling, go for it.

A study in the *Journal of Social and Personal Relationships* (yeah, we're backing this shit up with science too) found that people in rebound relationships actually reported higher self-esteem and emotional stability. The key is intentionality, if you're hoping this new person will heal you, validate you, or somehow fix your broken-ass self-esteem, you're setting yourself (and them) up for disaster.

YOUR STANDARDS HAVE CHANGED—THAT'S A GOOD THING

You're not the same person you were when got married. That's a win. After a divorce, most people report that their dating priorities shift. A 2021 study published in *Personal Relationships* found that divorced folks prioritize emotional stability, honesty, and shared values over hotness and spontaneity. Shocking, right? Turns out, getting burned once makes you less likely to put up with bullshit the second time around.

You probably also have a low tolerance for red flags now (more on red flags later). Good. Trust that. If someone seems like a manipulative liar on the first date, don't try to convince yourself they're just "mis-understood." You've seen this movie before, and it ends with you ranting to your therapist.

DATING APPS VS. OLD-SCHOOL DATING: WHAT'S YOUR POISON?

If your last dating experience was pre-smartphone era, congrats, you're about to experience the hellscape that is modern dating. Stanford University did a study in 2019 that found 39% of couples who got together in the past five years met online. So yeah, apps are a big deal. But that doesn't mean they don't suck.

- **Pros**: You have relatively endless options, can filter based on preferences, and you can avoid those awkward bar convos and ice breakers.
- **Cons**: Ghosting, fuckboys (and fuckgirls), scammers, and people who use 10-year-old profile pictures. Getting "catfished" is a real thing.

If the idea of swiping makes you want to light your phone on fire while it is still net to your face, try meetups or hobby groups or or even blind dates set up by friends. Worst case, you waste a night. Best case, you meet someone who isn't a dumpster fire.

Are You Actually Ready? Ask Yourself These Questions.
Before you throw yourself back into the dating pit, do a quick self-check:

- Am I dating because I want to, or because I feel like I "should"?
- Am I still emotionally wrecked?

- Have I dealt with my shit, or am I just looking for a distraction?
- Do I know what I want, and am I willing to walk away from someone who doesn't fit that?

Are You Actually Ready to Date After Divorce?
Don't Be the Trainwreck You're Attracted To

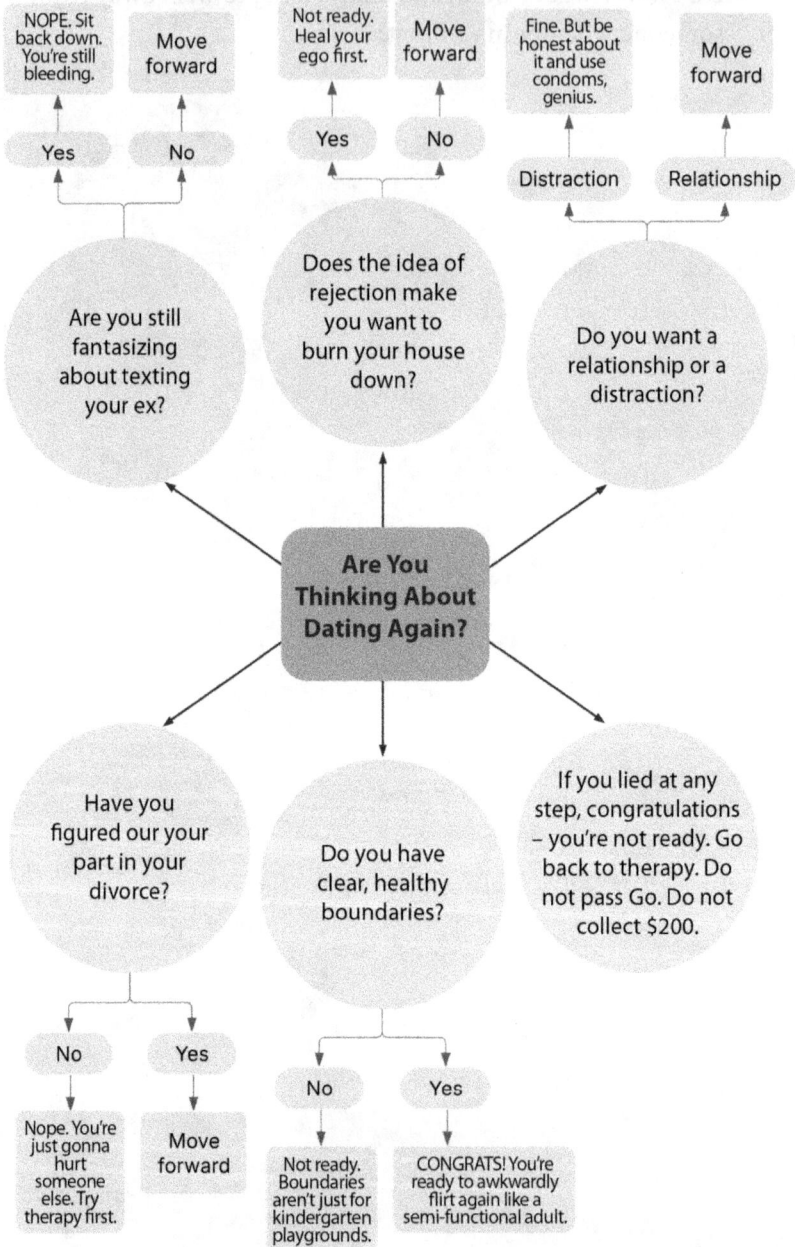

NOPE. Sit back down. You're still bleeding.

Move forward

Not ready. Heal your ego first.

Move forward

Fine. But be honest about it and use condoms, genius.

Move forward

Yes

No

Yes

No

Distraction

Relationship

Are you still fantasizing about texting your ex?

Does the idea of rejection make you want to burn your house down?

Do you want a relationship or a distraction?

Are You Thinking About Dating Again?

Have you figured our your part in your divorce?

Do you have clear, healthy boundaries?

If you lied at any step, congratulations – you're not ready. Go back to therapy. Do not pass Go. Do not collect $200.

No

Yes

No

Yes

Nope. You're just gonna hurt someone else. Try therapy first.

Move forward

Not ready. Boundaries aren't just for kindergarten playgrounds.

CONGRATS! You're ready to awkwardly flirt again like a semi-functional adult.

If you're just lonely, or worse, looking for revenge sex to "win" the breakup, pause. You don't need another person to fix your life. You need to handle your own shit first. Bringing someone else into your space when it is still cluttered with all the broken pieces of your past relationship isn't good for you, and it's a shitty thing to do to someone else.

Let's figure that out together, and for God's sake, wear a condom.

~Mustache Fun Fact:
A mustache can absorb 20% of its weight in beer. Drink responsibly.

MY STORY - THE FIRST DATE DISASTER

Alright, let's talk about the first date after divorce—because if you're anything like me, it's going to be a fucking catastrophe.

My first post-divorce date? Let's just say I was not ready. She had done some work with my department at the college, was young, very pretty, and always laughed at my jokes. I took a shot, and she decided to take a flyer on me. She was interested in getting to know who I was outside of work. Translation: she had no idea she was about to spend two hours with a broken, bitter man clinging to the wreckage of his former life.

I showed up wearing my best "I totally have my shit together" outfit. Having lost about 30 pounds since the divorce proceedings started, I was sure looking ready. Within ten minutes, I realized I was *not* ready and absolutely did *not* have my shit together.

· · ·

She asked normal, get-to-know-you questions. I, being emotionally stunted, answered them with sarcasm.

Her: "So, what do you like to do for fun?"

Me: "Mostly avoid my ex and workout until the pain inside dies down."

She laughed, which was a relief, but then she followed up immediately with "the "ex" question".

Her: "Do you still talk to your ex?"

My brain: OH SHIT. DEFLECT. ABORT.

Me: "Yeah, we have kids, so we communicate, poorly… mostly about how not to kill each other." Then I laughed at my own joke.

She blinked. Raised an eyebrow. I had immediately overstepped. Rookie mistake. Do not joke about homicide on a first date. The rest of the date? Painfully average. She was nice, but I was a walking red flag, and as we said goodbye, she smiled, turned to me, and said, "You'll get there. You're just… a little raw." Fucking. Ouch…

But she was right. I *was* raw. I was still piecing together who the hell I was outside of my marriage. And maybe, just maybe, I needed to figure that out before dragging someone else into the mess.

I needed to embrace my weirdness. Lean into it. I had to accept that there will be awkward moments, bad dates, and people who ghost me for no apparent reason. It's not a reflection of my worth, just as it is not a reflection of YOUR worth; it's just the game. Play it. Laugh about it, learn from it, and don't let one bad experience convince you that you're doomed to die alone surrounded by your dog and Amazon Prime delivery boxes.

GET YOUR HEAD RIGHT

Before you even think about downloading a dating app or saying yes to that coworker who's been eyeing you like a snack in the break room, you need to do a serious self-check. What's your motive? Where are you wanting this to go? Are you looking for connection, companionship, validation, a distraction, revenge sex, or just someone to split an Uber Eats order with? There's no wrong answer—just be honest with yourself.

If you're still emotionally bleeding out from your divorce, you're not ready. If the idea of your ex moving on fills you with blind rage, you're not ready. If you're convinced every potential partner is a manipulative, lying sack of garbage, you're not ready. Dating won't fix you. Only you can do that. Work through your anger, process your grief, and make peace with the fact that the past is done. You can still be angry, you can still be grieving, but they must be managed. Otherwise, you're just bringing your old shit into something new, and that's not fair to you or anyone else.

GREEN FLAGS (& RED ONES TOO!)

You spent years in a relationship that ended in flames. Learn from it. What did you like about your past relationship? What did you hate? What red flags did you ignore? What green flags did you take for granted? Make a list. No, seriously. Write that shit down. Not a fantasy list of unrealistic expectations (nobody's showing up with a seven-digit trust fund, six-pack abs, and a PhD unless you're on a reality show). Focus on the real stuff: honesty, kindness, emotional availability, a shared sense of humor. It's ok to have physical standards too, but don't get greedy. That fades over time anyway.

On the flip side, be clear about your deal-breakers. If you know you can't deal with someone who smokes, drinks excessively, or talks to their mother six times a day, don't pretend you can just because they're hot. Know your standards and stick to them.

TAKE IT SLOW (OR FAST... GO WITH WHAT YOU FEEL)

Some people want to wade back in slowly, dipping a toe into the dating pool. Others want to do a cannonball in pool yelling "LEROY JENKINS". Neither is wrong, as long as you're being honest with yourself and the people you're seeing.

If you just want to have fun (like sex), be upfront about it. That's what some other people want too. Nothing wrong with it. If you're looking for something serious, don't settle for someone who isn't. The key is clarity. You don't owe anyone a relationship, just like they don't owe you one. What you do owe them (and yourself) is honesty and respect.

REJECT REJECTION FEAR

You will get rejected. Period. No way around it. But here's the thing, rejection is not proof that you suck. It's just proof that you and that person weren't a match. That's it. It's a good thing. Move on.

Do not let rejection send you into a spiral of self-doubt. Do not let it convince you to lower your expectations or standards, and don't settle for something that doesn't make you happy. In the words of Roy Kent, "Don't you dare settle for *fine*!" You survived a divorce. You've already been through the worst kind of romantic rejection. A stranger on an app deciding they're not "feeling it" is nothing.

PROTECT YOUR PEACE

The best thing about dating after divorce is that you don't have to put up with bullshit anymore. You've been through enough. You know what you want. You know what you're worth. You don't need to tolerate flaky, dishonest, or emotionally unavailable people.

Your time is valuable. Your energy is valuable. If someone is draining you, stressing you out, or making you feel less than, cut them loose. You're not desperate. You're not running out of time. You're just getting started.

HAVE SEX, LOTS OF SEX (IF THAT'S YOUR THING)

Let's be real, sex is a big part of dating and might be the thing you're missing the most from when your marriage was working (if it was ever working). For many, sex with a partner they *actually* find attractive is a BIG benefit to this side of divorce. If you're ready and willing, go for it. You deserve pleasure, intimacy, and to feel desired. Just make sure you're doing it for the right reasons. Sure, sex can absolutely help you fill an emotional void, it is a hell of a revenge card to play, and it sure as hell works to boost the ego; but is that a good reason to start chucking wood at anyone willing to receive it? I'm not saying it's not a reason, I'm saying it wouldn't hurt to make sure it is a GOOD reason.

No matter where you land with your "reason" to start having sex again, once you start rocking that boat, PLEASE be safe. Use protection. Get tested. Have the awkward conversations about STDs, birth control, boundaries, and fetishes. If someone is weird about that, they don't deserve to be in your bed (on your couch, in your truck bed, etc.… you get the point). Consent isn't just about saying yes; it's about feeling understood, comfortable, respected, and in control. It is about active participation.

Also, sex is supposed to be fun. If it's stressful, shame-filled, or making you feel worse afterward, take a step back and reassess. Go back to "working on yourself" if you will (masturbation joke). This is your fresh start—you get to set the rules.

Sex Reentry Checklist:
Don't Be a Dumbass, Be a Safe, Satisfied Little Soldier

1. AM I OVER MY EX? ✔
    If you're still fantasizing about hate sex or revenge, you're not
    ready. Wait.
    Not today, Satan.

2. DO I ACTUALLY WANT SEX, OR AM I JUST
    LONELY/HORNY/BORED? ✔
    You can want it for fun, but don't lie to yourself about why
    you're doing it.
    Sex ≠ Emotional stability.

3. HAVE I TALKED TO A DOCTOR? ✔
    New chapter, new bloodwork. Get tested. Get clean. Be smart.
    Know your STD status before you go spelunking.

4. AM I EMOTIONALLY AVAILABLE ENOUGH TO NOT BREAK
    SOMEONE ELSE? ✔
    No one deserves to be your rebound trauma dump. Be honest,
    not a dick.
    Do no harm, take no shit.

5. DO I HAVE CONDOMS THAT AREN'T DUSTY AS HELL? ✔
    Your glovebox Trojans from 2015? Trash. Get fresh ones, use
    them.
    Wrap it before you tap it.

6. DO I KNOW MY BOUNDARIES AND KINKS? ✔
    You're allowed to want weird shit. Just know what it is and
    communicate like an adult.
    Safe words are sexy.

7. CAN I LAUGH IF THIS GETS WEIRD? ✔
    First sex after divorce might be awkward. Make it fun, not tragic.
    Awkward doesn't mean failure.

> *"This isn't about performance. It's about permission—
> to be safe, be seen, and get laid without losing yourself."*

MY STORY

By the time I got divorced, sex in my marriage was gone. I lost attraction to my ex-wife, and the idea of sex was something that caused me extreme anxiety. See, when I came home from Iraq, I struggled with some components in the bedroom. I don't know how much of it was chemical, and how much was mental, but I know that I was not as active or able as I was before. Talk about a kick to the self-esteem.

I tried medications, mindfulness, and had various medical issues that had contributed to the pitfalls of intimacy following my tour of service in the desert. Nothing seemed to work the same way it had before.

Fast-forward several years, and you can add a lack of attraction, a lack of emotional connection, and me feeling emotionally abused to the reasons I had to be fearful of sex with my partner. If there was any attempt to engage is a sexual relationship with my ex-wife where I was unable to perform, it went nowhere. Maybe it is because of the things she would say in those moments, and maybe it was because I was still working on my physical and mental health, but, it was rough.

Dating, and my relationships since the divorce have been a very different animal. People who care about you will not hold your experiences or your ailments you cannot control against you. Quite the opposite. Supportive, open, understanding, and emotionally intelligent people walk with you through your struggles when it comes to things like intimacy and sexual performance. I am very happy to report that that component of my life has been more fulfilling since my marriage ended than it ever was during my marriage. It is all about finding the right people or person for you and accepting people for who they are. Not what you want them to be.

NOW WHAT?

Reintegrating into dating after a messy divorce with someone who hurt you is a journey, not a sprint. You'll have good dates, bad dates, weird dates, and dates that make you question humanity. But every experience, even the bad ones, will help you figure out who you are and what you want. I had a Squad Leader in the Army who would say, "I learn something from all of you fuckers. Most of the time it is that you all had shitty parents." I think there is something in there about learning from the bad experiences too. So do that.

You're not the same person you were before your marriage. That's a good thing. You're wiser, stronger, and you've got stories to tell. So get out there. Have fun. Make mistakes. Just don't make the same ones twice (three times if she's hot). And above all, remember this: You are not broken. You are not unlovable. You are not too old or too damaged or too fucked up to find happiness again.

If nothing is working, give that mustache a try. You should've probably started with that. Now go get 'em, Sport.

~Iconic Mustache:
Tom Selleck insured his mustache for $1 million. Because true greatness deserves protection.

CHAPTER 8
CO-PARENTING AND PARALLEL PARENTING

So, you thought the divorce was the hard part? HA! Think again. Now, you get to raise kids with someone you'd rather never see again. Congratulations! You've unlocked the elite-level challenge of "co-parenting with the Devil". Buckle up, because this ride is bumpy, frustrating, and sometimes it will downright piss you off. But this chapter isn't about you. Your kids need you to figure this shit out, so let's get to work.

THE SOCCER GAME STANDOFF

Mark and Jessica had been divorced for almost a year, and their co-parenting relationship was a genuine disaster. Every conversation turned into a fight. If Mark said the sky was blue, Jessica would argue it was gray. It wasn't just about the big stuff, school choices, medical decisions, it was everything. There was no way, on this or any planet, that Mark and Jessica would agree. They hated each other. Visceral hate.

. . .

Then came the soccer game. Their eight-year-old son, Lucas, had his first tournament, and Mark had promised he'd be there. Jessica, on the other hand, had conveniently forgotten to tell Mark that Lucas needed new cleats. So, when Mark showed up, Lucas was in a brand-new pair of cleats that Jessica had bought without discussing it with Mark. When Mark got the chance to meet with his kiddo and tell him "good luck", Lucas made a passing comment about how "Mom said you probably wouldn't show up anyway."

That was it. Mark saw red.

Jessica smirked from the other side of the field, arms crossed, waiting for him to explode. He wanted to march over and tell her off, to call her out in front of everyone. He had proof she was poisoning their son against him. I've been where Mark was, and it sucks.

However, Mark would break out of his rage almost immediately when the crowd erupted, and Lucas ran up to him. "Dad! Did you see my goal?"

Right then, Mark had a choice: keep fuming about his horrible ex or focus on the reason he was actually there: his kid. So, he took a deep breath, smiled, and said, "Hell yeah, buddy. It was awesome."

Jessica still smirked. That's what Jessica did. But Lucas? Lucas beamed. And that made Mark happy.

That was the moment Mark realized co-parenting wasn't

about winning against his ex. It was about showing up for his kid, no matter how much bullshit he had to wade through to do it.

What's the lesson here?

Your ex might set traps. They might bait you. They might make you want to throw a folding chair across a soccer field (oof, been there). But your job isn't to fight them, it's to show up for your kid, every time, without fail. You don't have to like your ex. I think admitting that you don't like them is a great first step. But the next step is to be the best parent you can be in spite of them.

MY STORY

I wish I could tell you that I had the same restraint as Mark. I did not. See, there is a reason the book is "an Angry Ex-husband's Roadmap to Recovery", because I was really fucking angry. I was immature, I was jaded, and I was broken. Here comes that humility I've brought up a few times. I can recognize all of these things in myself and thank my therapist for help through them. But that's not how any of this started. It was bad. I was bad.

In the beginning, I struggled with a lot of resentment toward my ex. Co-parenting was difficult, and I had serious concerns about the differences in how we approached parenting. Our children's basic needs were being met. They had food, clothing, and were generally transported where they needed to go on time. In that sense, the essential responsibilities were covered.

Where we often clashed was in the less visible parts of parenting. Things like emotional support, consistency, and how discipline was handled. We did not see eye to eye on much, and that made things harder than they already were.

. . .

At the time, I said things out loud that were rooted in frustration. Some of what I said was too harsh. Some of it was fair. Most of it came from a place of exhaustion and grief. I will not pretend we were aligned in raising our kids, and I will not pretend that did not affect me. I also will not pretend that I always got it right.

There were things I wished she handled differently, especially when it came to how we interacted after the divorce. In my experience, communication was often difficult, and I found it hard to predict how she would respond to certain situations. There were moments when I felt like her actions created more tension than necessary, which made co-parenting even more challenging.

I have sometimes felt that our children's activities became a source of control or leverage rather than shared celebration. It also seemed like some of the legal filings came at moments when things were going well for me, which made them feel personal and intentionally disruptive. Whether that was her intent or not, it often felt like an attempt to undercut the progress I was trying to make in my own life.

I do not claim to know her motivations, but I know how those patterns affected me. They made recovery harder, and they made co-parenting more complex than it already was. That is my reality, and I am still learning how to manage it with as much grace and objectivity as possible.

My biggest mistake? Not letting any of that go early enough. I would never use the kids as leverage, but I did jump on every little mistake she made. I called her names, I critiqued things she did, and I made sure that she always knew how I felt about her. I never, in any capac-ity, said any of these things to or around the kids, but that didn't matter. I still needed to be better.

She took me to court, and I was held in contempt for unhealthy communication in a co-parenting relationship. Most of you are going through the thoughts in your mind that you've had about your ex right now, and you believe them to your core. Don't make my mistake. Control the distribution of these thoughts. I full sent everything. She had receipts.

Since all of this, I found that minimal interactions, Parallel Parenting (more on that later), and a co-parenting app was the best way for me to get better at co-parenting. It took me a long time, about four years, to buckle my behaviors up.

Do I still think and believe that she is not a good person? Of course! Don't be ashamed of your thoughts or feelings. Just keep them to yourself or share them with your FTB friends. You may think she deserves to hear how horrible she is. You might be right. Don't do it. It is financially not worth it.

SCOTT AND THE WHITE TIGER

Here is something one of my best friends, Scott, shared with me that helped me to reign in my anger.

The legendary duo of Siegfried and Roy put on a show for decades where they would make tigers and lions do all sorts of incredible feats for all to see. For more than three and a half decades, they had wild cats mesmerize audiences almost every day. At a show in 2003, their beloved white tiger, Manticore, attacked Roy and dragged him off stage where it took four crew members and a fire extinguisher to get the tiger to let him go. Thankfully, Roy survived.

Once recovered, and in solidarity with his lifetime performance partner, Siegfried, Roy issued a statement to any who would ask about the attack. See, the tiger was vilified in the news, and people were calling for the tiger to be put down. The duo met this anger with a simple statement along the lines of, "why are you mad at a tiger for acting like a tiger?". To the pair of wild cat tamers, the anomaly was that they performed for more than 36 years *without* a tiger attack.

Scott asked me the same question, in a way that made everything stick. At that time in the process, I thought my ex was a mean, and manipulative person. So he asked me why am I got mad when she acted mean and manipulative? That's like getting mad at a tiger for trying to eat someone. That's what tigers do.

It doesn't help to get mad at mean people when they're being mean. It is their norm. Express gratitude when they act in opposition of their typical behavior. That is a win to hold onto.

THE BASICS OF CO-PARENTING

Co-parenting, at its core, is about one thing: raising your children in a way that minimizes the damage from your divorce. Even perfect co-parents with happy and accommodating relationships deal with some damage to those kiddos. We need to mitigate that damage however possible. You and your ex don't have to like each other, I'm going to assume "like" is a far-off concept at this point, but you do have to communicate, coordinate, and at least pretend to be functional adults for the sake of your kids. Below are some principles that I am hopeful will give you some guidance. Some of it is hard to stomach, because it means having some personal accountability, but I'm telling you, those kids deserve the best. They didn't fuck up your marriage. You did, or she did, or you both did. Either way, they did NOT. Here we go.

It's Not About YOU!

As a therapist, I will always tell you that your feelings matter. Well, almost always. Because right here, your personal feelings toward your ex don't matter. Your job is to make sure your kids feel loved, supported, and secure. That means biting your tongue, keeping your emotions in check, and not using your kids as messengers, spies, or emotional support animals. Get a dog for that. You got the first step? Let's continue.

Communication is a Necessity (Not an Option)

You don't have to be best friends, but you do have to exchange information about your kids. It is going to be court ordered that you stay in constant communication about your children. That's what parents do. Your divorce doesn't change that. If direct conversation leads to screaming matches, then text. If texting your ex gives you hives because it is too immediate, use email. If that is still too difficult to keep things straight and organized, or even civil, there are amazing co-parenting apps like *OurFamilyWizard* or *TalkingParents*. These apps are well worth the investment! They even come with a "tone meter" to help you reword simple statements like "Hey, I know you're selfish, but the kids have a concert coming up." to "There is a concert coming up for the kids on (insert date here)." See? Both are true, but one is much safer to send. Bottom line here, if you want to communicate effectively, keep it factual, short, and devoid of any emotional jabs. Treat it like a business transaction with a terrible customer who spends tons of money at your store. You don't have to like them; you have to be a good businessman.

Communication Methods Pyramid

This pyramid shows the best to worst communication methods when dealing with a toxic ex. As you go up, your control, clarity, and emotional safety increase.

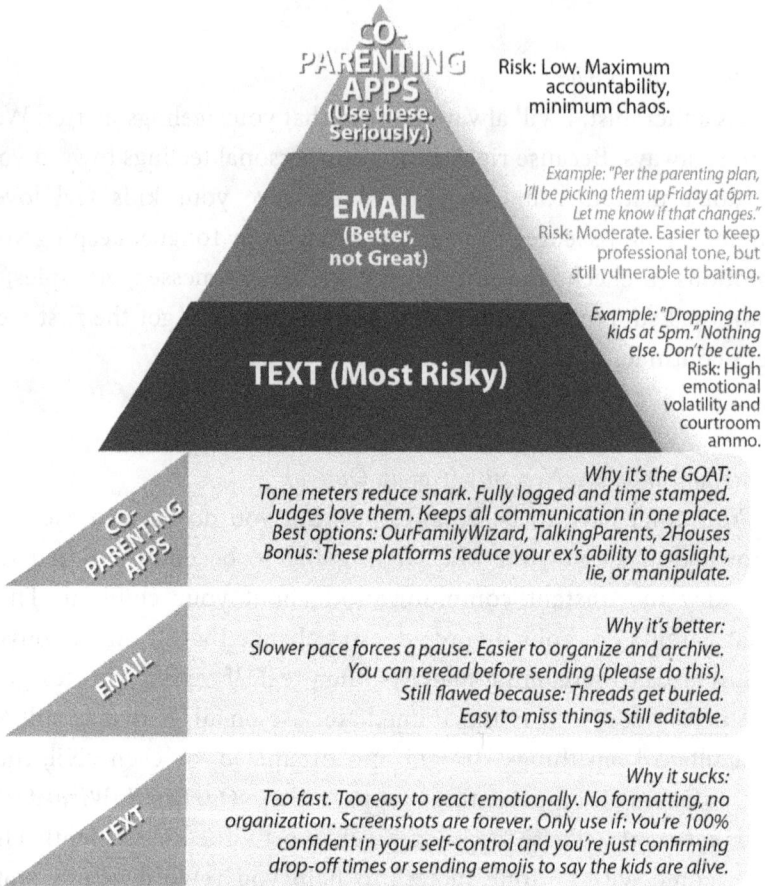

CO-PARENTING APPS (Use these. Seriously.)
Risk: Low. Maximum accountability, minimum chaos.

EMAIL (Better, not Great)
Example: "Per the parenting plan, I'll be picking them up Friday at 6pm. Let me know if that changes."
Risk: Moderate. Easier to keep professional tone, but still vulnerable to baiting.

TEXT (Most Risky)
Example: "Dropping the kids at 5pm." Nothing else. Don't be cute.
Risk: High emotional volatility and courtroom ammo.

CO-PARENTING APPS
Why it's the GOAT:
Tone meters reduce snark. Fully logged and time stamped. Judges love them. Keeps all communication in one place. Best options: OurFamilyWizard, TalkingParents, 2Houses
Bonus: These platforms reduce your ex's ability to gaslight, lie, or manipulate.

EMAIL
Why it's better:
Slower pace forces a pause. Easier to organize and archive. You can reread before sending (please do this). Still flawed because: Threads get buried. Easy to miss things. Still editable.

TEXT
Why it sucks:
Too fast. Too easy to react emotionally. No formatting, no organization. Screenshots are forever. Only use if: You're 100% confident in your self-control and you're just confirming drop-off times or sending emojis to say the kids are alive.

Bottom Line: The more conflict you have, the higher up the pyramid you need to be. Still texting your ex after she tried to subpoena your therapy notes? You're doing it wrong. Apps only. Protect your peace.

Consistency is Key

Kids thrive on routine. Work out a schedule that minimizes disruptions and stick to it (this isn't just for the kids either). The fewer surprises, the better. Whether it's school pick-ups, bedtime routines, or holiday plans, predictability helps kids feel safe. Kids deserve to feel safe. Especially while they are trying to navigate their new lives. Sure, two Christmases is pretty sweet, but right now they need two consistent parents.

Pick Your Battles

Not everything is worth a fight. Does it suck that your ex lets the kids eat junk food for dinner? Sure. Is it worth an all-out war? Probably not. Focus on the big stuff like education, health, and emotional well-being and learn to let go of the little things. I like to frame my thoughts on the court system. Are the kids fed? Sheltered? Safe? Are they being abused? If these are all satisfactory, then it's not worth your time or energy.

Stop Talking Shit!

No matter how tempting (or frankly, how easy) it is, don't do it. Kids absorb everything and hearing one parent bash the other can be really confusing. Your ex may be a raging dumpster fire, but your kids will figure that out on their own in time. Stay above it. Don't talk shit around your friends if the kids are there; don't talk shit about them on the phone in another room; hell, try to not talk shit in general. Save it for your therapist. The right therapist will even give you the space to get all that anger out.

Just. Not. Around. The. Kids!

~*Mustache Grooming:*
Invest in good scissors. Your stache deserves precision, not kitchen shears.

WHEN BASIC CO-PARENTING DOESN'T WORK: ENTER "PARALLEL PARENTING"

If you're dealing with an ex who thrives on conflict, refuses to cooperate, or turns every conversation into a war zone, co-parenting may be impossible. That's where parallel parenting comes in. Parallel parenting is like co-parenting's distant, emotionally detached cousin. It allows both parents to stay involved in their kids' lives while minimizing direct interaction. Some of you may want to start here. I'm just sayin. Here's how it works:

Communication Becomes Minimal and Structured

You only communicate when absolutely necessary and only about the kids. No personal chit-chat, no venting, no rehashing the past. Stick to emails, texts, or co-parenting apps (seriously, these apps are a life saver) and keep it brief and business-like. If you sit down and honestly ask yourself if you would want to have that person as your friend, and you answer "no", then stop trying to ask them about their day because you think you're supposed to. Direct. Minimal. Or Silence.

Each Parent gets to Parent Their Own Way

In traditional co-parenting, both parents try to align on rules and expectations. In parallel parenting, you accept that you have no control over what happens at your ex's house. They parent their way, you parent yours. As long as the kids are safe, you let it go. Don't spend time, energy, or resources trying to change anything. You do your best and hope the other parent is doing their best. Even though the way you both do things is DRASTICALLY different, if the children are safe, then let it be.

Document, Document, Document

If your ex is particularly difficult and mean, keep records of all communication. Stick to written formats and save messages in case you need to reference them later (or bring them to court). This protects you from false accusations and ensures accountability. Make sure you keep everything. With kids, you will communicate about a lot of stuff over time. Emails will get buried and finding old texts may result in you scrolling up on your phone for hours! Some folks find themselves in court without the ability to find old emails or texts while their partner is cherry picking emails to paint a pretty terrible picture. Trust me, it happens. Keep and organize EVERYTHING.

Accept that Peace is the Goal, Not Control

You won't win every battle. No major war in human history ended without each side losing battles. Your goal is to win the war on raising wonderfully adapted children. Some things will drive you crazy, but at the end of the day, your mental health, and your children's stability, matters more than proving a point to your ex. Learn to let go of what you can't change, and trust me, you can't change her.

THE REALITIES OF CO-PARENTING

Co-parenting is often painted as an ideal scenario where two mature adults set aside their differences and seamlessly work together for the benefit of their children. That's a nice fantasy. The reality of it sucks WAY more. But understanding the research behind co-parenting can help you navigate it with a little more clarity (and hopefully, fewer screaming matches).

1. The Psychological Impact of Divorce on Kids

- A study published in the *Journal of Family Psychology* found that children of divorced parents who engage in low-conflict co-parenting tend to fare significantly better in emotional regulation, academic performance, and social relationships than those caught in high-conflict arrangements.

- The biggest predictor of negative outcomes for children post-divorce? Parental conflict. It's not the divorce itself that screws them up—it's how the parents handle it.

2. Parallel Parenting vs. Co-Parenting

- Research suggests that parallel parenting—where parents disengage from each other and parent independently in their own homes—is actually better for children in high-conflict situations than forced co-parenting.
- A 2017 study from *Family Court Review* found that parallel parenting reduces children's exposure to conflict, which is critical for their long-term emotional stability.

3. The Role of Consistency

- Dr. Robert Emery, a leading expert in divorce psychology, emphasizes that consistency is more important than equal parenting time. Meaning, even if one parent has the kids more, as long as the routines are stable, the kids will adjust better.
- The National Institute of Child Health and Human Development suggests that predictability in parenting schedules helps children develop emotional security post-divorce.

4. Effective Communication Strategies

- A study in *Journal of Divorce & Remarriage* found that parents who use structured communication methods (like co-parenting apps) are 30% less likely to engage in conflict.
- Tools like OurFamilyWizard, TalkingParents, and 2Houses provide documented, neutral communication platforms, which can prevent the classic "he said, she said" bullshit from escalating into legal issues.

5. What NOT to Do: The Effects of Parental Alienation

- Parental alienation—when one parent manipulates the child against the other—has devastating psychological effects. Research in *Child and Adolescent Social Work Journal* found that children exposed to parental alienation exhibit higher rates of depression, anxiety, and relationship difficulties as adults.
- Simply put: Shit-talking your ex to your kids is emotional poison. They don't need to be your emotional support system, and they sure as hell don't need to hear how much you hate their mother.

Co-parenting with a difficult ex is exhausting and sometimes downright impossible. But you're not in this for revenge, you're in it for your kids. Whether you can make co-parenting work or need to make the switch to parallel parenting, the goal is the same: providing a safe, stable, loving environment for your children. They didn't screw this up. So don't screw them up. You can't change your ex, if you could, you wouldn't be divorced, but you can control how you react.

. . .

Be the bigger person, set firm boundaries, and focus on your kids.

That, and your new mustache, are the real wins here.

~Mustache Folklore:
In some cultures, mustaches symbolize wisdom. In others, badassery. Coincidence? Probably not.

CHAPTER 9
GETTING OUT ALIVE

If you're still here, congratulations! You've survived the wreckage. Maybe you're still pulling shards of your old life out of your ass, but guess what? You made it. I knew you would (ehh…) And now, the other side of all this bullshit is waiting for you. The storm, however destructive, doesn't last forever. The clouds part. The sun comes out. And when it does, life is brighter, sharper, and, dare I say it, better.

THE BIGGEST JOKER OF ALL: TIME

Time is an asshole. During trauma, it drags. Every minute feels like an hour of agony, every day an eternity of suck. But here's the kicker, on the other side, once you start healing, time speeds back up again. Research backs this up: our perception of time warps during traumatic events. The brain, in survival mode, processes everything in excruciating detail, making moments feel longer. But as we recover, as we start to re-engage with life, time begins to move at a normal (sometimes even breakneck) pace. The takeaway? When you're in the depths of hell, it feels like forever. It's not. Hold on. The clock keeps ticking, and eventually, it works in your favor.

LEARN AND APPLY CHAPMAN'S 5 LOVE LANGUAGES

I used to think love was about saying "I love you" a lot and not cheating. That was it. Say the magic words, boom! relationship 101. But somehow, every woman I dated still ended up pissed off, distant, or crying over wine with their friends named Amanda. Then I read Gary Chapman's *The 5 Love Languages*, and it hit me like a slap from a woman who's been "fine" for three weeks straight.

Turns out, love isn't one-size-fits-all. People feel loved in different ways. There are five main ones, and if you're speaking the wrong damn language, you might as well be shouting sweet nothings in Klingon. Below is a quick breakdown to help you on the backend of all of this.

Words of Affirmation

This one's for the people who need to *hear* it. Not just "I love you" once a year like a Hallmark zombie, but "you're amazing," "I appreciate you," "damn, you handled that well." If your partner lights up when you compliment them, this is probably their jam. Forget this and you're basically starving them emotionally.

Acts of Service

Love isn't talk; it's doing the dishes without being asked. It's picking up her prescription on the way home. If your partner melts when you take something off their plate (figuratively, not their literal dinner), this is their love language. Screw this one up and you're the roommate who also sleeps in their bed.

Receiving Gifts

No, it's not about being a gold-digging troll. It's about thoughtfulness. The small things that say, "I saw this and thought of you." Could be a latte, a keychain, or that stupid little trinket they mentioned once six months ago. If you keep forgetting birthdays and anniversaries, guess what? You're speaking gibberish.

Quality Time

Put the damn phone down. This one's about being present. No distractions, no bullshit. If your partner gets giddy just hanging out and talking, this is their language. Ignore them while scrolling TikTok and you might as well just tell them to go love themselves.

Physical Touch

Not just sex (though yeah, that counts). Hugs. Handholding. Random back rubs. If your partner's constantly touching you like a human security blanket, touch is their currency. Neglect this one and you'll end up cuddling your cold, lonely ego.

Bottom line? Learn these languages or watch the love die a slow, quiet death. Don't be that clueless schmuck wondering what went wrong while you next partner packs their bags. Pick up the Chapman book and read it for yourself. Now is the exact time for you to start figuring this shit out.

JOHN GOTTMAN'S FOUR HORSEMEN OF THE RELATIONSHIP APOCALYPSE

Once you learn your love languages, put them into practice, and start building your next relationship, it is vitally important that you understand how to recognize real relationship killers. Not infidelity. Not financial stress. Not even your mother-in-law inserting herself like Michael Cera in a mustache growing contest. No, according to Dr. John Gottman (a dude who can predict divorce with scary accuracy), there are four toxic behaviors that ride in like the goddamn apocalypse and absolutely *wreck* your love life. Maybe this information would've been nice to have a year ago, but oh well. We are working your new life from today forward.

He calls them the Four Horsemen. I call them "How to Fuck Up a Relationship in Four Easy Steps."

Criticism

This one feels normal because we all do it. But there's a difference between saying, "Hey, can you take out the trash?" and "You *never* take out the trash because you're lazy and selfish." See the difference? One is a request; the other is an attack on their personality. Criticism isn't feedback, it's verbal shrapnel. Keep throwing it around, and they'll start emotionally ducking every time you open your damn mouth.

Contempt

Oh, this one's the nuclear option. Eye-rolling, sarcasm, sneering, talking down like you're better than them. This is the *fuck you* energy that kills intimacy faster than a surprise colonoscopy. Gottman says this is the biggest predictor of divorce, and he's not guessing. Contempt doesn't just hurt feelings, it straight-up erodes the soul. If you catch yourself mocking your partner like they're beneath you, congratulations, you're the asshole.

Defensiveness

This is what you do when you're too chicken shit to own your part. Your partner says, "Hey, that hurt my feelings," and you come back with, "Well maybe if you weren't so sensitive!" Instead of listening, you build a wall. A big, dumb, emotional wall with barbed wire made of excuses. The more defensive you get, the more they feel like they're screaming into a void. You're not protecting yourself; you're just refusing to grow.

. . .

Stonewalling

This is the emotional version of walking out of the room and slamming the door. Except you stay *in* the room, you just go dead inside. You shut down, tune out, give the cold shoulder. It's like talking to a warm corpse. And spoiler: nobody wants to be in a relationship with a goddamn ghost.

So, if you see these four bastards showing up in your relationship, don't ignore them. They don't just crash the party; they burn the whole damn house down. Name them when you see them. Call them out. And for the love of whatever sanity you've got left, *do the work* before the next love you try to build gets trampled.

LOVE, SEX, & THE MYTH OF MONOGAMY

One of the most toxic beliefs we're fed from childhood is that we're supposed to find "The One." That one person who completes us, who sticks around through everything, who is our ride-or-die. Sounds great in theory. In practice? Not so much.

Data suggests that monogamy, as we practice it, is a pretty terrible investment. The divorce rate hovers around 40-50% in many parts of the world, and even the "successful" marriages often involve some level of dissatisfaction, infidelity, or quiet misery. Studies on long-term relationships indicate that sexual and emotional satisfaction tends to decline over time, and many people simply stay together out of kids, obligation, financial entanglement, or sheer inertia.

So, what's the alternative? Maybe it's embracing a broader, more flexible view of relationships as you move forward. Ethical nonmonogamy, open relationships, or simply the acknowledgment that love and connection don't have to fit a rigid, one-size-fits-all model. The goal isn't to mimic a societal standard that clearly doesn't work for a huge chunk of us, it is to find what actually makes you happy. And that starts with knowing yourself and being brutally honest about what you want.

Myth	Reality
"True love lasts forever."	Love changes. People grow (or don't). Forever is rare, not automatic.
"If it's real, it should be easy."	Relationships are hard. Effort isn't a flaw–it's the point.
"Sex stays exciting forever with the right person."	Without intention and communication, even porn stars get bored.
"Jealousy = Love."	Jealousy = Insecurity. Love = Trust and autonomy. Different things.
"Marriage fixes everything."	Marriage magnifies whatever bullshit was already there.
"Monogamy comes naturally."	It doesn't. It's a choice. A DAILY choice, not a biological default.
"If they cheat, they never loved you."	Love and loyalty are separate skills. People can love you and still suck at loyalty.
"Being single means you failed."	Being miserable in a relationship is failure. Single can mean strength.
"You're not broken because you didn't get a fairy tale. Fairy tales are for kids and liars."	

MY STORY

Here I am, writing a book, more than six years after my divorce. I have built successful mental health practices, I have enjoyed dating, and I have built a life I can be proud of. My relationship with my kids is amazing. This process has been challenging, and I have fallen on my face over and over and over again. But my recovery from this is not defined by the falls, rather it is defined by my ability to learn from whatever tripped me.

My life has a lot of years left. I plan to keep messing up and learning. I plan to love deep and hard. I might even plan to try and have a more productive working relationship with my ex (don't hold your breath on this one). What I can absolutely guarantee is that I am better now than I ever was in my marriage.

I am more confident. I have better friendships. I have a job and a purpose that I love. I understand what I want in an intimate and romantic relationship. ALL these things happened because I was sent through hell, fought every fucking demon that stepped into the ring with me, and walked out burnt. But I sure as hell walked out.

You will too.

~Mustache Records:
The longest mustache ever measured was over 14 feet. Ambitious goals start small.

ENJOY YOURSELF, TAKE YOUR TIME, & BE AUTHENTIC

The biggest mistake people make after divorce is rushing. Rushing into another serious relationship. Rushing into defining themselves by someone else. Rushing to prove they're "over it." You don't have to do any of that.

Take your time. Learn to enjoy your own company. Go on dates if you want. Sleep around if that feels right. Stay single if that's what makes you happy. The only thing that matters is that whatever you're doing, you're doing it authentically.

Authenticity is the real goal. When you've spent years being who someone else wanted you to be, it takes effort to find your real self again. Strip away the expectations, the conditioning, the bullshit. Ask yourself: Who am I, really? What do I actually want? And once you figure that out, don't compromise. The whole point of surviving this mess is to create a life that's actually yours. One that's full, still probably a little messy, joyful, passionate, and real.

The Authenticity Compass: Find Your Real North

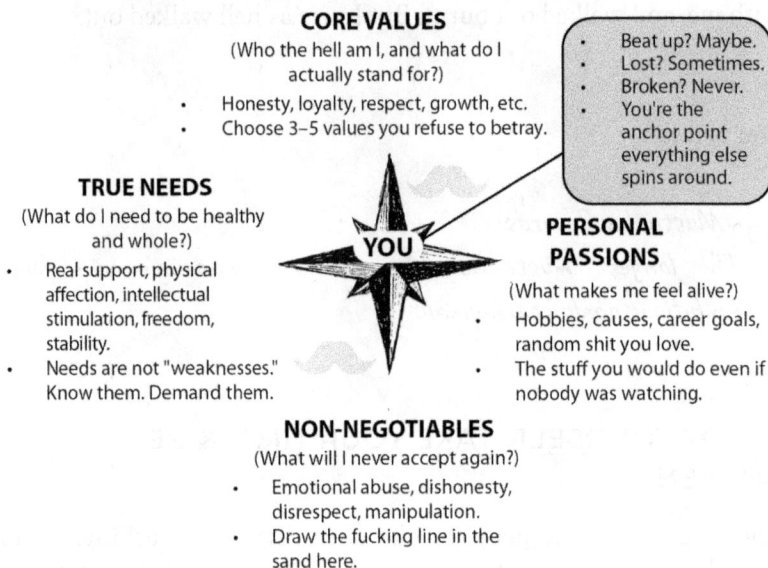

CORE VALUES
(Who the hell am I, and what do I actually stand for?)
- Honesty, loyalty, respect, growth, etc.
- Choose 3–5 values you refuse to betray.

- Beat up? Maybe.
- Lost? Sometimes.
- Broken? Never.
- You're the anchor point everything else spins around.

TRUE NEEDS
(What do I need to be healthy and whole?)
- Real support, physical affection, intellectual stimulation, freedom, stability.
- Needs are not "weaknesses." Know them. Demand them.

YOU

PERSONAL PASSIONS
(What makes me feel alive?)
- Hobbies, causes, career goals, random shit you love.
- The stuff you would do even if nobody was watching.

NON-NEGOTIABLES
(What will I never accept again?)
- Emotional abuse, dishonesty, disrespect, manipulation.
- Draw the fucking line in the sand here.

> "You don't find yourself after divorce. You rebuild yourself, brick by brick."
> Decorations: Maybe a cracked heart symbol, some arrows, or a faint doodle of a mustache as the compass arrowhead.

You got out of the storm you beautiful mustached bastard. Now go live.

~Mustache Maintenance:
Wax isn't optional. Unless your goal is chaos—then by all means, proceed.

REFERENCES

Amato, Paul R. "The Consequences of Divorce for Adults and Children." Journal of Marriage and Family, vol. 62, no. 4, 2000, pp. 126-149.

American Psychological Association. The Role of Social Support in Coping with Divorce. APA, 2021, www.apa.org/topics/divorce/social-support.

Bernet, William, et al. "Parental Alienation, DSM-5, and ICD-11: Response to Critics." Child and Adolescent Social Work Journal, vol. 37, no. 3, 2020, pp. 315-330.

Blustein, David L., et al. "The Role of Work in Psychological Health and Well-being: A Conceptual, Historical, and Public Policy Perspective." Journal of Occupational Health Psychology, vol. 24, no. 1, 2019, pp. 1-18.

Coleman, Marilyn, and Lawrence Ganong. Family Estrangement: Theories, Assessment, and Intervention. Springer, 2018.

Emery, Robert E. The Truth About Children and Divorce: Dealing with the Emotions So You and Your Children Can Thrive. Viking, 2004.

Fisher, Bruce. Rebuilding: When Your Relationship Ends. Impact Publishers, 2016.

Gottman, John, and Nan Silver. The Seven Principles for Making Marriage Work: A Practical Guide from the Country's Foremost Relationship Expert. Harmony, 1999.

Holmes, Thomas H., and Richard H. Rahe. "The Social Readjustment Rating Scale." Journal of Psychosomatic Research, vol. 11, no. 2, 1967, pp. 213-218.

Kelly, Joan B., and Robert E. Emery. "Children's Adjustment Following Divorce: Risk and Resilience Perspectives." Journal of Family Psychology, vol. 15, no. 3, 2003, pp. 355-370.

Knapp, Mark L., and Anita L. Vangelisti. Interpersonal Communication and Human Relationships. Pearson, 2013.

Kross, Ethan, et al. "Social rejection shares somatosensory representations with physical pain." Proceedings of the National Academy of Sciences, vol. 108, no. 15, 2011, pp. 6270-6275.

Kubler-Ross, Elisabeth. On Death and Dying. Scribner, 1969.

Lehmiller, Justin. The Psychology of Human Sexuality. Wiley-Blackwell, 2017.

Marriage.com. "Divorce Statistics and Facts: What Affects Divorce Rates in the U.S.?" Marriage.com, 2023, www.marriage.com/advice/divorce/divorce-statistics-and-facts/.

McCarthy, Robert J., and Amanda J. Landers. "Friendship Loss and Divorce: A Longitudinal Analysis." Social Psychological and Personality Science, vol. 12, no. 3, 2020, pp. 351–367.

McDermott, Ryan C., et al. "Rebound Relationships: Evaluating Relationship Quality, Need Fulfillment, and Psychological Distress in New Romantic Relationships After a Breakup." Journal of Social and Personal Relationships, vol. 31, no. 4, 2014, pp. 511-533.

Meyer, Rebecca. "Post-Divorce Family Dynamics and Social Disconnection." Journal of Divorce & Remarriage, vol. 63, no. 2, 2022, pp. 85-102.

Neff, Lisa A., and Benjamin R. Karney. "How Stress Buffers and Erodes Romantic Relationships." Current Directions in Psychological Science, vol. 16, no. 3, 2007, pp. 128-132.

Parker, Emily R., et al. "Emotional Resilience and Social Networks Post-Divorce." Journal of Divorce & Remarriage, vol. 61, no. 4, 2019, pp. 273-290, www.tandfonline.com/journal/jdmr.

Pruett, Marsha Kline, et al. "Enhancing Father Involvement in Divorce: Promoting Healthy Coparenting and Father–Child Relationships." Journal of Divorce & Remarriage, vol. 53, no. 2, 2012, pp. 267-285.

Rosenfeld, Michael J., et al. "Disintermediating Your Friends: How Online Dating in the United States Displaces Other Ways of Meeting." Proceedings of the National Academy of Sciences, vol. 116, no. 36, 2019, pp. 17753-17758.

Saxbe, Darby E. "A field (researcher's) guide to cortisol: Tracking HPA axis functioning in everyday life." Health Psychology Review, vol. 2, no. 2, 2008, pp. 163-190.

Sbarra, David A., and Jessica L. Coan. "Divorce and health: Current trends and future directions." Psychosomatic Medicine, vol. 80, no. 9, 2018, pp. 742-743.

Simpson, Jeffry A., and W. Steven Rholes. Attachment Theory and Close Relationships. Guilford Press, 1998.

Smith, John P. "Psychological Recovery and Friendship: The Buffering Effect of Social Networks After Major Life Transitions." American Journal of Sociology, vol. 124, no. 2, 2018, pp. 431–458, www.journals.uchicago.edu/doi/full/10.1086/701232.

Sullivan, Michael J. "Coparenting and Custody Conflict: Findings and Implications for Family Court." Family Court Review, vol. 48, no. 1, 2010, pp. 45-58.

Vrticka, Pascal, et al. "Neural processing of social emotion in attachment insecurity: An fMRI study." Human Brain Mapping, vol. 34, no. 7, 2013, pp. 1887-1896.

Wagner, Ursula, et al. "Beautiful friendship: Social sharing of emotions improves subjective feeling and objective well-being." Journal of Experimental Social Psychology, vol. 50, 2014, pp. 642-648.

Weiss, Robert S. Marital Separation. Basic Books, 1975.

About the Publisher
TACTICAL 16

Tactical 16 Publishing is an unconventional publisher that understands the therapeutic value inherent in writing. We help veterans, first responders, and their families and friends to tell their stories using their words.

We are on a mission to capture the history of America's heroes: stories about sacrifices during chaos, humor amid tragedy, and victories learned from experiences not readily recreated — real stories from real people.

Tactical 16 has published books in leadership, business, fiction, and children's genres. We produce all types of works, from self-help to memoirs that preserve unique stories not yet told.

You don't have to be a polished author to join our ranks. If you can write with passion and be unapologetic, we want to talk. Go to Tactical16.com to contact us and to learn more.

All of Tactical 16's books are available on our online bookstore, T16Books.com. Visit it today to see more books from our selection of authors and to find a new adventure to read!

www.ingramcontent.com/pod-product-compliance
Lightning Source LLC
Chambersburg PA
CBHW070126030426
42335CB00016B/2281